KNITS **MEN** WANT

The 10 Rules Every Woman Should Know Before Knitting for a Man

PLUS THE ONLY 10 PATTERNS SHE'LL EVER NEED

Bruce Weinstein

Photographs by

JARED FLOOD

STC CRAFT | A MELANIE FALICK BOOK | NEW YORK

To Mark, who wears everything I knit for him.

Published in 2010 by Stewart, Tabori & Chang
An imprint of ABRAMS

Text copyright © 2010 by Bruce Weinstein
Photographs copyright © 2010 by Jared Flood

Library of Congress Cataloging-in-Publication Data

Weinstein, Bruce, 1960-
    Knits men want / by Bruce Weinstein ; photographs by Jared Flood.
        p. cm.
    ISBN 978-1-58479-840-8
    1. Knitting. 2. Men's clothing. I. Title.
    TT825.W453 2010
    746.43'2--dc22   2009035053

Editors: Liana Allday and Melanie Falick
Designer: Susi Oberhelman
Production Manager: Jacqueline Poirier

The text of this book was composed in Berthold Akzidenz Grotesque and Mercury.

Printed and bound in China
10 9 8 7 6 5 4 3 2 1

Stewart, Tabori & Chang books are available at special discounts when purchased in quantity for premiums and promotions as well as fundraising or educational use. Special editions can also be created to specification. For details, contact specialsales@abramsbooks.com or the address below.

115 West 18th Street
New York, NY 10011
www.abramsbooks.com

Contents

Introduction

It's 6 p.m. on a Thursday evening in early fall. My class at Sit-N-Knit, a spacious and welcoming yarn shop in Bloomfield, Connecticut, is filling up—ten women have come to learn how to knit sweaters from the top down. Each one is knitting a sweater for herself, and each seems to have a sad story to tell about her experiences knitting for a man in her life. None of them are eager to try again; I'm hoping to change a few minds.

I always bring food to class. It helps everyone relax, gets people talking, and ensures they'll all come back week after week no matter how frustrated they might be with their sweaters or how little progress they may have made. On the menu this week is a three-layer coconut cake from my latest cookbook.

Around the table everyone is eating, casting on, and sharing their stories. Mary says she's hesitant to make anything for her husband since the first sweater she knitted for him ended up at the Salvation Army. I don't know how, but she recounts the story with a smile and great humor. Irma says her husband begs her to bake cakes like mine, but she's on strike since he doesn't appreciate her knitting. Barbara is *wearing* a sweater she made for her husband. I hear their tales and encourage them to keep knitting for their guys. But regardless of their talent, I realize that these women have some homework to do before they will be able to create garments the men in their lives will want to wear: They first have to understand the male psyche.

Over the years, many women have knitted beautiful items for their boyfriends, husbands, sons, brothers, fathers, and uncles, only to have the goods packed away in drawers never to see the light of day.

Disappointing? Yes. Frustrating? Certainly. But is a man who does this being intentionally insensitive? Is he trying to push his girlfriend's buttons? Is he holding out for something more exciting from his wife in bed? Not at all.

When men don't wear what women make them, they're just being men—with their own quirky likes and dislikes and an inability to express them. When they abuse the garments knitters make them, they're still just being men—hardwired *not* to think about feelings, *not* to think about how much work went into making them, and *not* understanding why their behavior is so upsetting. Women can't expect to change these male characteristics, but they can change what they choose to make for the men in their lives.

As a rule, most men don't read *Vogue*, window shop, or care about fashion. They don't know what's in style and, in most cases, they don't care. While women know that fashions change and that beauty has its price, men don't pay attention to any of it. Men like three things: simple designs, muted colors, and soft fabrics. And to hell with what the magazines, fashion columns, and yes,

But if women want to succeed at knitting for men, they're going to have to find a way to extract this information from the male brain.

Now, before you give up on knitting for men altogether, know that help is on the way. As a man, I know what men like and don't like, which gives me a genetic edge that most knitters don't have. And as a knitting instructor, I am equipped to be your translator, and to help you match your knitting skills with what the men in your life really want. (For starters—here's an easy one—nix the knitted iPod, golf club, and beer cozies.)

I learned to knit from my grandmother, a dressmaker by trade. She worked for top designers in New York City, creating samples from sketches. Her creations were exclusively for women and always *au courant*. During her off hours, she knitted exclusively for men: me, my brother, and my cousin. These creations were anything but trendy. They were dark, simple sweaters that we wore and loved. My grandmother knew what worked for men and it had nothing to do with her personal taste or what she created for runway models.

Only once did my grandmother knit me a sweater that I refused to wear, and in all honesty, I asked for it. On my first day of college, I befriended the woman sitting next to me in graphic design class. Her name was Rainey Day (yes, that is her real name). I fell in love with her Bing-cherry tinted hair and her hip-length tunic sweater with wide horizontal ribs that started at the bottom hem and went all the way up to the oversized turtleneck. She told me she designed and knitted the sweater and I immediately asked to borrow it. I took it to my grandmother and begged her to make me one.

even their women, tell them they should wear. What this means is that your man will rarely pick out the same pattern and yarn for himself that you would pick out for him. And what makes this situation even more challenging is that men don't communicate as well as women do, so you'll rarely get him to tell you up front what he likes.

"Nice work," she said, "but why do you want a woman's sweater?"

I was young, thin, and in art school, and it seemed like a good idea at the time. Looking back, I realize that I wanted that sweater as a work of art, not as a piece of clothing. My grandmother made the sweater in my size and by the time she'd finished it I had to admit that, despite my bohemian attitude, I would never wear it. I've kept that sweater to this day, partly because I feel guilty all these years later that I made her work so hard on a sweater that I never put on and partly because it's my own personal time capsule of the late 1970s. But it's also a good reminder for me of how easy it is to veer off course if you aren't careful.

The truth is that women often make sweaters that their guys are not comfortable wearing. They use colors that are too bright, make the cables too wide, or choose buttons and zippers that are just too flashy. How does this happen? Well, some women have told me that they find

Women and Men: A Side-by-Side Comparison

WOMEN	MEN
Women love to impress, stand out in a crowd.	Men love to blend in, not call attention to themselves.
Women love to shop and are looking for what's in style today.	Men hate to shop and prefer clothing that will be in style forever.
A woman will dress up for any occasion.	A man will dress up for his wedding and his funeral.
Women wear socks below their ankles with fuzzy balls on them.	Men do not wear socks below their ankles with fuzzy balls on them.
Women know what colors go well together.	If a man likes two colors, why can't they go together?
Women will skip lunch to afford a new outfit.	Men will wear an old outfit to take a woman to lunch.
Women like clothing to look cute.	Men like clothing to look cute—on women.

most men's patterns boring, so they adapt them from women's patterns to add a little more interest. The "interest" that is added, however, is often totally inappropriate, like feminine stitchwork and edgings. Other women insist that they won't touch dark, drab colors, period. So they choose bright colors that are more fun to knit with. But the fault doesn't just rest on the knitter here. Many women claim that they can't get their guy to turn away from a football game long enough to look at yarn samples. And men love to rely on revisionist history—when asked if they like something, guys will say *sure, sure* without even looking up, only to complain later that they don't remember being offered a choice. The first trick to finding the right pattern for your guy is striking a balance between patterns that are fun and interesting to knit while still being simple and classic enough for a man to wear. The second is learning to communicate what you intend to make for him every step of the way.

To that end, I'm sharing ten rules that will help you knit successfully for all the men in your life. Some of these rules may strike you as overgeneralizations, but I assure you that men, no matter their lifestyle, are fairly consistent. In fact, these rules even apply to the president of the United States (see below). Following each rule is a corresponding pattern that should please you and your guy, such as a two-tone cotton baseball jersey with a wide saddle shoulder (see page 82), and a basic hooded sweatshirt (see page 68) that is so soft yet easy to take care of, your man can roll it in a ball and shove it under the bed and it will still look great when he takes it out to wear.

The patterns are written to be worked in multiple gauges for almost any yarn to fit nearly every man. So you can knit the same sweater for your guy whether he's tall and skinny or built like a linebacker. And why only ten patterns? Because when it comes to fashion, that's all any man wants or needs. When a man finds what he likes, he sticks with it. It's not uncommon for a guy to have three or four of the same sweater crammed into a drawer. If he wants variety, he might have it in black, navy, and dark gray, and when one sweater wears out, he's likely to buy the same exact sweater to replace it. And while this book may not erase the pain of handknits past, I hope that these insights and patterns will add joy to your knitting—and to your relationships with men—from this page forward.

President Obama Proves My Point

After throwing out the first pitch at the 2009 Major League Baseball All-Star Game in what were later deemed "mom jeans" by the media, Barack Obama told Meredith Viera on the *Today* show, "I'm a little frumpy." He went on to say that the way he looked didn't bother him in the least (Rule #9: Men are Oblivious), that he hates to shop (Rule #4: Men Hate Fittings), and finally, "Those jeans were comfortable" (Rule #7: Men Are Babies). Sound familiar?

Men Can't Fake It

SKI **SWEATER**

Men can't fake it. Not in bed or anywhere else. Take him to the ballet on the night of a championship basketball game and he won't even pretend to enjoy himself. Same story if you knit him a sweater he doesn't like—he may put it on once or twice to please you, but ultimately, it's destined for the back of the drawer or the charity pile.

Mary, a knitting instructor at my local yarn shop, learned her lesson the hard way. Her husband, Larry, doesn't like wearing anything bulky so she chose a thin yarn for a new sweater for him. Maybe it was her tension with the yarn—possibly even some subconscious tension she had with Larry—but she turned out a sweater that was so stiff, it nearly stood by itself on the floor without any visible means of support. Needless to say, Larry wasn't interested in the full body cast she had whipped up for him.

Mary acknowledged that she had missed on the gauge, but she was determined to try again. This time she would surprise Larry with "lots of fancy stitchery" in an alpaca-wool blend that was warm enough for him to wear without a coat.

"So how did it go over?" I asked, as she recounted the story to me one afternoon at the shop.

"He gave it to the Salvation Army." He thought it had too many cables, too much ornamentation, too much going on.

Mary was frustrated, but she didn't give up. For her next attempt, she brought Larry to the yarn shop (a wise move), where he chose a dark box-pattern pullover on display.

"Did you make it for him?" I said.

"Yes," Mary said. "It's gorgeous. Dressy."

"And?"

"He wore it to rake leaves," Mary said with some disdain.

"It bothered you that he *wore* it?"

"It's too nice to wear raking leaves," she said. "He can rake the leaves in a crummy old sweater."

"Did you make him go inside and change?"

"No, I had to let him wear it. What else could I do?"

At this point, I told Mary the four words that might change her relationship with Larry forever—"What's it to you?"

If Larry—or any man—wants to rake leaves wearing cashmere, let him do it. If he wants to rake leaves wrapped in cellophane, let him do it. Knitting a sweater that a man wants to wear isn't an easy task, so take your successes where you can get them. In fact, rejoice in them.

Picking Men's Patterns: A Basic Playbook

- Keep it simple. Most men want functional clothing—not works of art.

- If a pattern calls for fringe, scallops, picot, or other fancy edgings or includes words like butterfly, popcorn, bobble, daisy, brocade, tulip, eyelet, or lace, take another look at the picture. Are you sure this is a man's pattern?

- Stick to stitch patterns with words like stockinette, rib, chevron, and herringbone in them. But remember to keep chevrons small and in similar tones—no man wants to look like Charlie Brown.

- Keep cables narrow. Most men think wide cables are feminine, but narrow cables are acceptable.

- Beware of neck styles. Shawl collars can be too feminine for many men and rolled necks can work with younger guys but are not usually favored after a certain age. To be safe, stick to crewneck or V-neck styles.

- Think under the rainbow—most men want to live in Kansas, not Oz. Choose subdued colors over brights. Guys usually prefer solid colors—two colors max.

- Stick with finer, smooth yarns—about 4 stitches to the inch or more. Guys tend to like the machine-made look these yarns can offer.

- Most men don't like anything heavy or bulky under their coats, so either pick lightweight yarns for sweaters or make heavier sweaters that can be worn on their own.

- Check your pattern's schematic measurements and choose a size that fits his frame. Bulky, oversized garments sometimes suit lanky, young guys, but once a man has "filled out," they may just make him feel (and look) fat.

- Buttons can make a statement, just be careful how strong a statement. Buy a few choices and show them to your guy before you sew them on.

- For sweaters that require zippers, choose ones with an antiqued or matte finish, avoiding anything shiny.

- Don't make matching outfits for men and their children or pets—ever.

- Avoid costumes. If it looks like it could have come from a collection at the Metropolitan Museum of Art, it's a pass.

SKI **SWEATER**

This sweater is the softest and warmest garment in the collection. The baby alpaca will keep your guy comfortable on the slopes or shoveling the driveway without a coat. The sides are slightly tapered as the sweater descends, accentuating the chest and shoulders while minimizing the waist.

Sizes	Small (Medium, Large, X-Large, 2X-Large, 3X-Large)
Finished Measurements	40 (44, 48, 52, 56, 60)" chest
Notions	Stitch holders
Stitch Patterns	**Half Fisherman's Rib** (multiple of 2 sts; 2-row repeat) **Row 1 (WS):** Knit. **Row 2:** *K1b, p1; repeat from * to end. Repeat Rows 1 and 2 for Half Fisherman's Rib. **1x1 Rib** (multiple of 2 sts; 1-rnd repeat) **All Rnds:** *K1, p1; repeat from * to end.
Notes	This pattern is customizable for multiple sizes and multiple gauges. First make a Half Fisherman's Rib swatch with the yarn you are using to determine appropriate gauge. Then determine the finished chest measurement you want. To make it easier to follow the pattern, you might want to highlight all the numbers that pertain to your chosen gauge and size. The pattern calls for slipping the first stitch of every row. This gives you a clean selvage for sewing this sweater together, keeping your rib intact all around. Just remember to slip that stitch every time, on every piece.

Yarn Requirements

GAUGE	FINISHED CHEST MEASUREMENT					
	40	**44**	**48**	**52**	**56**	**60"**
3	1345	1490	1710	1880	2090	2250 yards
3½	1505	1685	1905	2125	2330	2535
4	1675	1865	2120	2345	2585	2800
4½	1835	2050	2325	2585	2835	3075
5	2005	2220	2530	2800	3090	3340
5½	2175	2425	2735	3045	3325	3605
6	2335	2600	2940	3265	3610	3880

Back

FINISHED CHEST MEASUREMENT					
40	**44**	**48**	**52**	**56**	**60"**

Back

CO

GAUGE						
3	58	64	70	76	82	88 sts.
3½	66	74	80	88	94	102
4	76	84	92	100	108	116
4½	86	96	104	114	122	132
5	96	106	116	126	136	146
5½	104	116	126	138	148	160
6	114	126	138	150	162	174

Row 1 (WS): Slip 1, work Half Fisherman's Rib to last st, k1.

Row 2: Slip 1, work to last st, p1.

Work even until piece measures 3" from the beginning, ending with a WS row.

SHAPE BODY

Increase Row (WS): Increase 1 st each side this row, then every

GAUGE	
3	0" (all sizes)
3½	6
4	6
4½	6
5	6
5½	4
6	4

GAUGE	
3	0 time(s), as follows: Slip 1, M1, work to last st, M1, k1.
3½	1
4	1
4½	1
5	1
5½	2
6	2

Total sts:

	40	44	48	52	56	60
3	60	66	72	78	84	90 sts.
3½	70	78	84	92	98	106
4	80	88	96	104	112	120
4½	90	100	108	118	126	136
5	100	110	120	130	140	150
5½	110	122	132	144	154	166
6	120	132	144	156	168	180

Work even until piece measures 15½ (16, 16, 16, 16½, 16½)" from the beginning, ending with a WS row. Place marker either end of row for beginning of armhole. Work even until armhole measures 10 (10½, 11½, 12½, 13, 13½)" from the beginning, ending with a WS row.

SKI SWEATER SHOWN ON FACING PAGE.

SIZE: Small; **FINISHED MEASUREMENTS:** 40" chest; **YARN:** Misti Alpaca Chunky (100% baby alpaca; 108 yards / 100 grams): 14 hanks #M321 Blue & Charcoal; **NEEDLES:** One pair straight needles size US 8 (5 mm), one 16" (40 cm) long circular (circ) needle size US 8 (5 mm). Change needle size if necessary to obtain correct gauge. **GAUGE:** 18 sts and 16 rows = 4" (10 cm) in Half Fisherman's Rib

SHAPE NECK AND SHOULDERS

GAUGE

	40	44	48	52	56	60"
Next Row (RS): At beginning of next 2 rows, BO						
3	19	22	24	27	29	32 sts.
3½	22	26	28	32	34	38
4	25	29	32	36	39	43
4½	28	33	36	41	44	49
5	31	36	40	45	49	54
5½	34	40	44	50	54	60
6	37	43	48	54	58	64
Place remaining sts on holder for Back neck:						
3	22	22	24	24	26	26 sts.
3½	26	26	28	28	30	30
4	30	30	32	32	34	34
4½	34	34	36	36	38	38
5	38	38	40	40	42	42
5½	42	42	44	44	46	46
6	46	46	48	48	52	52

GAUGE

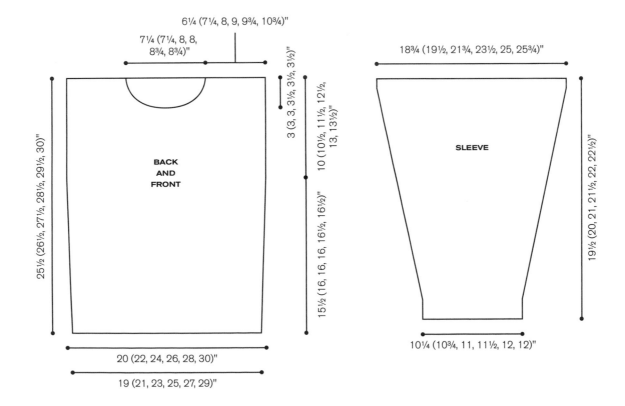

6¼ (7¼, 8, 9, 9¾, 10¾)"

7¼ (7¼, 8, 8, 8¾, 8¾)"

3 (3, 3, 3½, 3½, 3½)"

10 (10½, 11½, 12½, 13, 13½)"

BACK AND FRONT

25½ (26½, 27½, 28½, 29½, 30)"

15½ (16, 16, 16, 16½, 16½)"

20 (22, 24, 26, 28, 30)"

19 (21, 23, 25, 27, 29)"

18¾ (19½, 21¾, 23½, 25, 25¾)"

SLEEVE

19½ (20, 21, 21½, 22, 22½)"

10¼ (10¾, 11, 11½, 12, 12)"

Front | Work as for Back, beginning Body shaping at 6" instead of 3", until armhole measures 7 (7½, 8½, 9, 9½, 10)", ending with a WS row.

SHAPE NECK

FINISHED	CHEST	MEASUREMENT			
40	**44**	**48**	**52**	**56**	**60"**

Next Row (RS): Work

GAUGE

	40	44	48	52	56	60"
3	22	25	28	31	33	36 sts,
3½	26	30	33	37	39	43
4	30	34	37	41	44	48
4½	34	39	42	47	50	55
5	37	42	47	52	56	61
5½	41	47	52	58	61	67
6	45	51	56	62	67	73

join a second ball of yarn, work the following sts, then place on holder for Front neck:

GAUGE

	40	44	48	52	56	60"
3	16	16	16	16	18	18 sts,
3½	18	18	18	18	20	20
4	20	20	22	22	24	24
4½	22	22	24	24	26	26
5	26	26	26	26	28	28
5½	28	28	28	28	32	32
6	30	30	32	32	34	34

work to end. Working both sides at the same time, BO 2 sts each neck edge

GAUGE

	40	44	48	52	56	60"
3	0	0	1	1	1	1 time(s),
3½	1	1	2	2	2	2
4	1	1	1	1	1	1
4½	2	2	2	2	2	2
5	2	2	2	2	2	2
5½	2	2	3	3	2	2
6	3	3	3	3	3	3

then decrease 1 st each neck edge every other row

GAUGE

	40	44	48	52	56	60"
3	3	3	2	2	2	2 time(s).
3½	2	2	1	1	1	1
4	3	3	3	3	3	3
4½	2	2	2	2	2	2
5	2	2	3	3	3	3
5½	3	3	2	2	3	3
6	2	2	2	2	3	3

Work even until piece measures same as for Back to shoulders. BO all sts.

Sleeves | Sew shoulder seams. With RS facing, pick up and knit the following sts between armhole markers:

GAUGE

	40	44	48	52	56	60"
3	56	60	66	70	74	76 sts.
3½	66	70	76	82	86	88
4	76	80	88	94	98	102
4½	84	90	98	106	110	114
5	94	100	108	118	122	126
5½	104	110	120	130	134	138
6	112	120	130	142	148	152

Row 1 (WS): Slip 1, work Half Fisherman's Rib to last st, k1.
Row 2: Slip 1, work to last st, p1.
Work even for 1", ending with a WS row.

	FINISHED	CHEST	MEASUREMENT			
	40	**44**	**48**	**52**	**56**	**60"**

SHAPE SLEEVE

Next Row (RS): Decrease 1 st each side this row, every

GAUGE

	40	**44**	**48**	**52**	**56**	**60"**
3	10	8	8	8	6	6 rows
3½	10	8	8	8	6	8
4	10	8	8	6	6	6
4½	10	8	8	6	6	6
5	10	8	8	6	6	8
5½	10	8	8	6	6	8
6	10	8	8	6	6	6

GAUGE

	40	**44**	**48**	**52**	**56**	**60"**
3	1	8	5	0	14	14 time(s),
3½	1	10	7	0	19	0
4	1	12	7	22	22	22
4½	5	14	9	25	25	25
5	4	16	12	28	28	1
5½	4	18	11	31	31	1
6	8	20	14	33	34	35

then every

GAUGE

	40	**44**	**48**	**52**	**56**	**60"**
3	8	6	6	6	4	6 rows
3½	8	6	6	6	4	6
4	8	6	6	4	4	4
4½	8	6	6	4	4	4
5	8	6	6	4	4	6
5½	8	6	6	4	4	6
6	8	6	6	4	4	4

GAUGE

	40	**44**	**48**	**52**	**56**	**60"**
3	9	4	9	16	3	3 time(s).
3½	11	4	9	19	1	20
4	13	4	12	0	1	2
4½	10	4	12	0	1	2
5	13	4	11	0	1	28
5½	15	4	15	0	1	31
6	12	4	14	1	1	1

Remaining sts:

GAUGE

	40	**44**	**48**	**52**	**56**	**60"**
3	34	34	36	36	38	40 sts.
3½	40	40	42	42	44	46
4	46	46	48	48	50	52
4½	52	52	54	54	56	58
5	58	58	60	60	62	66
5½	64	64	66	66	68	72
6	70	70	72	72	76	78

Work even until piece measures 19½ (20, 21, 21½, 22, 22½)", or to desired length from pick-up row. BO all sts in pattern.

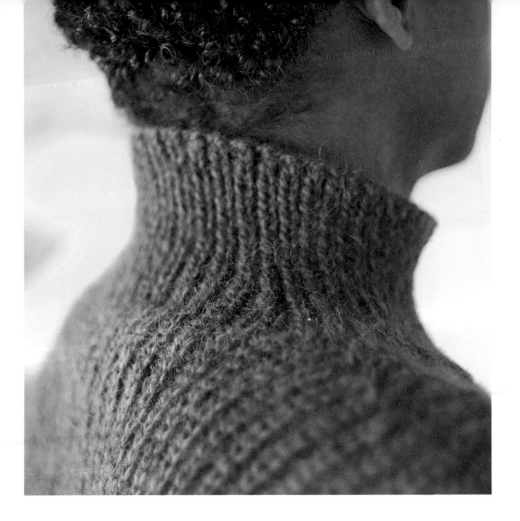

Finishing

Block as desired. Sew side and Sleeve seams.

COLLAR

GAUGE

	FINISHED CHEST MEASUREMENT					
	40	**44**	**48**	**52**	**56**	**60"**

Using circular needle, beginning at left shoulder, pick up and knit the following sts, including sts on holders:

GAUGE	40	44	48	52	56	60"
3	60	60	64	68	72	72 sts.
3½	72	72	76	80	84	84
4	82	82	86	92	96	96
4½	94	94	98	104	108	108
5	106	106	108	116	120	120
5½	116	116	118	126	132	132
6	128	128	132	140	146	146

NOTE: *You may need to adjust the number of sts you pick up between sts on holders so that when you work the ribbing across the sts on holders, you maintain the look of the pattern from the body across sts on holders.* Begin 1x1 Rib; work even for 4 (4, 4½, 4½, 5, 5)", or to desired length. BO all sts in pattern.

Men **Resist** Change

It's a fundamental truth that men don't make over their wardrobes as often as women do. Therefore, even if your taste or knitting skills evolve, it does not mean that his taste in fashion will evolve at the same pace.

What you must remember is this: If he's over 15, he's probably got his style locked in—and he likes it. Men get into comfortable ruts and comfortable sweaters and don't want to get out of them. So if he knows what he likes, get used to it.

I noticed this rule in action one day as I sat with Mark at Le Gamin, a Parisian-style café

in the heart of Chelsea, New York City's gallery district. It was late March and still snowing, but inside the café, with knitting on my lap, I felt warm and comfortable. I was working on a sweater for Mark. The cleaners had lost his favorite pullover and he had asked me for another one. Same style. Same color.

In the back corner sat Ethan Hawke and his young son, both drinking hot chocolate. I seemed to be the only one starstruck in the place. I couldn't even get Mark's head out of the manuscript he was editing to pay attention to my sighting.

But, finally, he did look up when I asked for an opinion on Ethan's sweater, which was light brown and so tight you could make out his internal organs.

"Make mine bigger," Mark said and then went back to his work.

I couldn't decide if Ethan's tight sweater was high fashion or simply an old favorite that he had outgrown years ago, but couldn't part with. Either way, I was making Mark's bigger, exactly like the one he had lost.

Between the two of us and the movie star sat our friend Jack and his "salon," a group of intellectuals who gathered each week to discuss the current woes of the city—how expensive parking had gotten in Chelsea, why co-op boards were always raising maintenance fees. Jack held court in a time warp where nothing changed, from his sermons on 1960s government conspiracies to his wardrobe, which that particular Friday featured the same sweater he'd worn for years: a thin merino crewneck in navy blue stockinette stitch, with a plain T-shirt underneath. I'd seen Jack in that sweater hundreds of times over the years.

Understanding His Style: DOs and DON'Ts

DO	DON'T
Go through his wardrobe and look for a theme. Then make him something similar to what he already has.	Hesitate to repeat styles; just change the color from one shade to another.
Take your man shopping and ask him to point out clothing that appeals to him. It's easier for a man to show you what he likes than to describe it off the top of his head. And if getting your guy to go shopping is out of the question, try flipping through catalogues on the couch.	Ask him to describe why he doesn't like to wear a certain style. While women might enjoy this question, most men rank it up there with What are you thinking?, another female favorite.
Accept his taste as it is and adjust your knitting accordingly.	Ask for advice from his mother or your girlfriends.

Jack's wife, Kerry, was on her way to the café to knit with me but as usual she was late, probably taking the afternoon to rip out any mistakes from her previous evening's knitting group. Kerry believes that knitting is sacred and ripping, if it must be done, is a private matter—not to be undertaken in public. So I ordered a croissant, continued knitting the sweater at hand, and waited.

When Kerry finally arrived, she squeezed into the banquette beside me.

"How can you knit that same sweater over again?" she asked, reaching for a bite of my croissant. "You should knit Mark a Fair Isle or Aran sweater."

Mark looked up and told her that he liked what I was making.

"But aren't you bored with it?"

I love her dearly, but this is an ongoing debate between us. Kerry is not willing to knit anything that doesn't challenge her. I love a good challenge, but if I offer to make something for a friend and he or she picks a project that might be a little dull to knit, I'll do it anyway.

Kerry's tea arrived and she settled into the afternoon's task: weaving in the ends of a multicolored, striped alpaca turtleneck. It was very stylized, like something out of Italian *Men's Vogue*.

"Who's that for?" I asked.

"Jack."

I looked from the sweater in her hands to Jack in his favorite plain sweater and was dumbstruck. "*That* Jack," I wanted to say, but kept my mouth shut and pondered.

Finally, I turned to Kerry and said, "Slip it on. Let me see."

I saw Jack glance adoringly across the café at his wife as she tried on the ornate sweater she was knitting for him. And I thought to myself—how lucky it is that Kerry and Jack wear the same size.

BASIC **PULLOVER** AND **VEST**

This flexible pattern includes instructions for knitting a basic sweater at six different gauges, in six different sizes and with the choice of two necklines: crewneck and V-neck. It also includes instructions for a vest variation. So, no matter your man's preferences, you're covered. The sleeve is designed with a modified drop shoulder that is "set in" just slightly to offer your guy a flattering and comfortable fit. It's attractive on any man's physique as it makes the shoulders appear broad and the waist seem small.

Sizes	Small (Medium, Large, X-Large, 2X-Large, 3X-Large)
Finished Measurements	40 (44, 48, 52, 56, 60)" chest
Notions	Stitch marker
Stitch Pattern	**1x1 Rib** (multiple of 2 sts; 1-row/rnd repeat) **All Rows/Rnds:** *K1, p1; repeat from * to end.
Notes	This pattern is customizable for multiple sizes and multiple gauges, and includes instructions for crewneck and V-neck versions. First make a Stockinette stitch swatch with the yarn you are using to determine appropriate gauge. Then determine the finished chest measurement you want. To make it easier to follow the pattern, you might want to highlight all the numbers that pertain to your chosen gauge and size.

PULLOVER SHOWN ABOVE.
SIZE: Large; **FINISHED MEASUREMENTS:** 48" chest; **YARN:** O-Wool Classic (100% organic merino; 198 yards / 100 grams): 9 hanks #4303 Evergreen; **NEEDLES:** One pair straight needles size US 8 (5 mm), one 16" (40 cm) long circular (circ) needle size US 8 (5 mm). Change needle size if necessary to obtain correct gauge. **GAUGE:** 18 sts and 28 rows = 4" (10 cm) in Stockinette stitch (St st)

Yarn Requirements

		FINISHED CHEST MEASUREMENT					
		40	44	48	52	56	60"
Pullover	3½	1125	1245	1395	1525	1615	1720 yards
GAUGE	4	1255	1370	1535	1675	1785	1900
	4½	1380	1520	1695	1850	1960	2095
	5	1505	1645	1835	2000	2140	2250
	5½	1620	1795	1995	2180	2320	2470
	6	1745	1910	2145	2340	2495	2635
Vest	3½	670	765	850	955	1020	1125 yards
GAUGE	4	745	835	935	1045	1130	1235
	4½	815	925	1030	1160	1240	1370
	5	885	995	1115	1245	1350	1470
	5½	960	1095	1205	1365	1465	1605
	6	1030	1160	1300	1460	1575	1715

Back

CO

GAUGE		40	44	48	52	56	60"
	3½	62	70	76	82	90	96 sts.
	4	72	80	86	94	102	110
	4½	80	90	98	106	114	124
	5	90	100	108	118	128	136
	5½	98	110	120	130	140	150
	6	108	120	130	142	154	164

Begin 1x1 Rib; work even until piece measures 2 (2, 2, 2½, 2½, 2½)" from the beginning, ending with a WS row, increase the following sts evenly spaced across last row:

GAUGE		40	44	48	52	56	60"
	3½	8	8	8	10	8	10 sts.
	4	8	8	10	10	10	10
	4½	10	10	10	12	12	12
	5	10	10	12	12	12	14
	5½	12	12	12	14	14	16
	6	12	12	14	14	14	16

Total sts:

GAUGE		40	44	48	52	56	60"
	3½	70	78	84	92	98	106 sts.
	4	80	88	96	104	112	120
	4½	90	100	108	118	126	136
	5	100	110	120	130	140	150
	5½	110	122	132	144	154	166
	6	120	132	144	156	168	180

Next Row (RS): Change to St st; work even until piece measures 16 (16½, 16½, 17, 17, 17½)" from the beginning, ending with a WS row.

SHAPE ARMHOLE

Next Row (RS): At beginning of next 2 rows, BO

GAUGE	40	44	48	52	56	60"
3½	6	9	9	12	15	18 sts.
4	7	10	11	14	17	20
4½	8	11	12	16	19	23
5	9	12	13	18	21	26
5½	10	13	15	20	23	28
6	11	15	16	21	25	31

Remaining sts:

GAUGE	40	44	48	52	56	60"
3½	58	60	66	68	68	70 sts.
4	66	68	74	76	78	80
4½	74	78	84	86	88	90
5	82	86	94	94	98	98
5½	90	96	102	104	108	110
6	98	102	112	114	118	118

Work even until armhole measures 9 (9½, 10½, 11½, 12, 12½)", ending with a WS row.

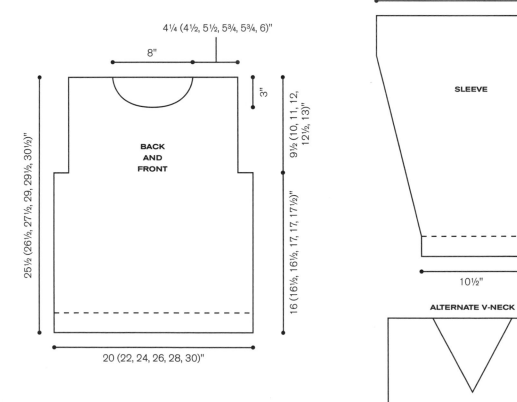

4¼ (4½, 5½, 5¾, 5¾, 6)"

8"

3"

9½ (10, 11, 12, 12½, 13)"

BACK
AND
FRONT

25½ (26½, 27½, 29, 29½, 30½)"

16 (16½, 16½, 17, 17, 17½)"

20 (22, 24, 26, 28, 30)"

19 (20, 22, 24, 25, 26)"

SLEEVE

24 (24½, 25½, 26, 26½, 26½)"

10½"

ALTERNATE V-NECK

7 (7, 7, 7½, 7½, 7½)"

SHAPE SHOULDERS AND NECK

	FINISHED CHEST MEASUREMENT					
	40	**44**	**48**	**52**	**56**	**60"**
Next Row (RS): Work						
3½	15	16	19	20	20	21 sts,
4	17	18	21	22	23	24
4½	19	21	24	25	26	27
5	21	23	27	27	29	29
5½	23	26	29	30	32	33
6	25	27	32	33	35	35

GAUGE

GAUGE	40	44	48	52	56	60"

join a second ball of yarn, BO center

GAUGE						
3½	28 sts (all sizes), work to end.					
4	32					
4½	36					
5	40					
5½	44					
6	48					

Working both sides at the same time, work even until armhole measures 9½ (10, 11, 12, 12½, 13)", ending with a WS row. BO all sts.

Front
Crewneck Version

Work as for Back until armhole measures 6½ (7, 8, 9, 9½, 10)", ending with a WS row.

SHAPE NECK

Next Row (RS): Work

GAUGE						
3½	22	23	26	27	27	28 sts,
4	25	26	29	30	31	32
4½	28	30	33	34	35	36
5	31	33	37	37	39	39
5½	34	37	40	41	43	44
6	37	39	44	45	47	47

join a second ball of yarn, BO center

GAUGE						
3½	14 sts (all sizes), work to end.					
4	16					
4½	18					
5	20					
5½	22					
6	24					

Working both sides at the same time, work even for 1 row.

Next Row (RS): BO 3 sts each neck edge once, 2 sts once, then decrease 1 st each neck edge every other row

GAUGE						
3½	2 times (all sizes).					
4	3					
4½	4					
5	5					
5½	6					
6	7					

Remaining sts each shoulder:

GAUGE						
3½	15	16	19	20	20	21 sts;
4	17	18	21	22	23	24
4½	19	21	24	25	26	27
5	21	23	27	27	29	29
5½	23	26	29	30	32	33
6	25	27	32	33	35	35

work even until armhole measures 9½ (10, 11, 12, 12½, 13)", ending with a WS row. BO all sts.

| **Front** | Work as for Back until armhole measures 2½ (3, 4, 4½, 5, 5½)", ending with a WS row. |
| **V-Neck Version** | **Next Row (RS):** Work to center, join a second ball of yarn, work to end. Work even for 1 row. |

FINISHED CHEST MEASUREMENT

	40	**44**	**48**	**52**	**56**	**60"**

SHAPE NECK

Next Row (RS): Working both sides at the same time, decrease 1 st each neck edge this row, then every other row

GAUGE	
3½	13 times (all sizes).
4	15
4½	17
5	19
5½	21
6	23

Remaining sts each shoulder:

GAUGE	40	44	48	52	56	60
3½	15	16	19	20	20	21 sts.
4	17	18	21	22	23	24
4½	19	21	24	25	26	27
5	21	23	27	27	29	29
5½	23	26	29	30	32	33
6	25	27	32	33	35	35

Work even until armhole measures 9½ (10, 11, 12, 12½, 13)", ending with a WS row. BO all sts.

Sleeves

CO

GAUGE	
3½	36 sts (all sizes).
4	42
4½	46
5	52
5½	56
6	62

Begin 1x1 Rib; work even until piece measures 2 (2, 2, 2½, 2½, 2½)" from the beginning, ending with a WS row, increase the following sts across last row:

GAUGE	
3½	4 sts (all sizes).
4	4
4½	6
5	6
5½	8
6	8

Total sts:

GAUGE	
3½	40 sts (all sizes).
4	46
4½	52
5	58
5½	64
6	70

	40	44	48	52	56	60"

SHAPE SLEEVE

Next Row (RS): Change to St st, increase 1 st each side this row, every 6 (4, 4, 2, 2, 2) rows

GAUGE

	40	44	48	52	56	60"
3½	7	0	10	0	4	10 times,
4	9	0	10	0	4	10
4½	10	0	12	0	3	12
5	12	0	12	0	5	13
5½	10	0	15	0	5	15
6	12	0	14	0	5	15

then every 8 (6, 6, 4, 4, 4) rows

GAUGE

	40	44	48	52	56	60"
3½	5	14	8	21	19	15 times.
4	5	16	10	24	22	18
4½	6	18	11	27	26	20
5	6	20	13	30	28	22
5½	9	22	13	33	31	24
6	9	24	16	36	34	27

Total sts:

GAUGE

	40	44	48	52	56	60"
3½	66	70	78	84	88	92 sts.
4	76	80	88	96	100	104
4½	86	90	100	108	112	118
5	96	100	110	120	126	130
5½	104	110	122	132	138	144
6	114	120	132	144	150	156

Work even until piece measures 24 (24½, 25½, 26, 26½, 26½)" from the beginning, or to desired length, ending with a WS row. BO all sts.

Finishing

Block as desired. Sew shoulder seams. Sew in Sleeves. Sew side and Sleeve seams.

Crew Neckband

Using circular needle, pick up and knit the following sts around neck shaping:

GAUGE

3½	72 sts (all sizes).
4	82
4½	92
5	104
5½	114
6	124

Join for working in the rnd; place marker (pm) for beginning of rnd. Begin 1x1 Rib; work even for 1". BO all sts in pattern.

V-Neckband

Using circular needle, pick up and knit the following sts around neck shaping, making sure to pick up 1 st at bottom center of Front neck:

GAUGE

3½	86	86	86	90	90	90 sts.
4	98	98	98	102	102	102
4½	110	110	110	114	114	114
5	124	124	124	128	128	128
5½	136	136	136	140	140	140
6	148	148	148	154	154	154

Join for working in the rnd; pm for beginning of rnd.

Decrease Rnd: Begin 1x1 Rib; work to 1 st before center st, s2kp2, work to end.

Repeat Decrease Rnd every rnd until Neckband measures 1¼". BO all sts in pattern.

MAKE IT A VEST | Work as for Sweater to beginning of armhole shaping.

	FINISHED	CHEST	MEASUREMENT			
	40	**44**	**48**	**52**	**56**	**60"**

SHAPE ARMHOLES

Next Row (RS): At beginning of next 2 rows, BO

GAUGE	40	44	48	52	56	60"
3½	4	5	7	8	9	10 sts.
4	4	6	8	9	10	12
4½	5	7	9	10	11	13
5	6	8	10	11	12	14
5½	6	9	11	12	13	16
6	7	9	12	13	15	17

Decrease 1 st each side this row, then every other row

GAUGE	40	44	48	52	56	60"
3½	2	3	2	4	5	7 times.
4	3	0	0	5	7	8
4½	3	4	4	6	8	10
5	3	5	5	7	9	12
5½	4	5	6	8	11	13
6	5	7	6	9	11	15

Remaining sts:

GAUGE	40	44	48	52	56	60"
3½	52	56	60	62	64	66 sts.
4	60	64	68	70	72	74
4½	68	72	76	80	82	84
5	76	78	84	88	92	92
5½	84	88	92	98	100	102
6	90	94	102	106	110	110

Work even until armhole measures 8¾ (9¼, 10¼, 11¼, 11¾, 12¼)", working back neck shaping of Crewneck or V-Neck shaping as for Sweater, ending with a WS row. NOTE: *Because armhole shaping (and the resulting number of shoulder sts) is different for the Vest than for the Sweater, you will need to place markers on either side of the center neck sts before beginning neck shaping.*
Next Row (RS): Continuing with neck shaping, decrease 1 st each side this row, then every other row once.
Work even until armhole measures same as for Sweater.

Finishing | Block as desired. Sew shoulder seams. Sew side seams. Work Neckband as for Sweater.

ARMHOLE EDGING

Using circular needle, pick up and knit the following sts around armhole shaping:

GAUGE	40	44	48	52	56	60"
3½	74	78	86	96	102	106 sts.
4	84	90	100	110	116	122
4½	94	102	112	124	130	138
5	104	112	124	136	144	152
5½	114	124	138	150	158	168
6	126	134	150	164	174	184

Join for working in the rnd; pm for beginning of rnd. Begin 1x1 Rib; work even for ¾". BO all sts in pattern.

VEST SHOWN ABOVE.

SIZE: Large; **FINISHED MEASUREMENTS:** 48" chest; **YARN:** Jo Sharp Silkroad DK Tweed (85% wool / 10% silk / 5% cashmere; 147 yards / 50 grams): 7 balls #408 Cedar; **NEEDLES:** One pair straight needles size US 8 (5 mm), one 16" (40 cm) long circular (circ) needle size US 8 (5 mm). Change needle size if necessary to obtain correct gauge. **GAUGE:** 18 sts and 26 rows = 4" (10 cm) in Stockinette stitch (St st)

Men Sweat

BASIC **CARDIGAN** TWO WAYS

For years I sang with choruses that performed at Carnegie Hall in New York City. The dress code for all concerts was black tie. I liked putting on a tux every few months for an evening on the town, that is, until I was blasted by the hot stage lights. By the middle of the program, I, along with the rest of the bass and tenor sections—the men—would be wet and pungent. We all brought dry shirts to change into during intermission.

I was always amazed that the altos and sopranos—the women—were never visibly sweating. Not once do I recall a woman wiping her brow during a performance or changing her shirt during intermission. Yet the lights were just as hot on their side of the stage.

Curious to know why men sweat more than women do, I did some research at The National Library of Medicine website. I learned that humans have all sorts of sweat glands, but surprisingly, women have more of the basic sweat glands than men. Despite that fact, women still sweat less, in part, because they use these sweat glands more efficiently than men do.

Adding to the problem for men is the fact that they have larger apocrine sweat glands. Apocrines are triggered by emotional stimuli as well as heat, and they produce the kind of sweat that stinks.

So what gets a man so nervous he sweats? Well, many men worry about sweating too much in the first place, which might explain why some men avoid sweaters altogether or don't seem quite as appreciative as one would think they ought to be when gifted with one. (Think about it—even the name of this garment evokes the problem.)

The flip side to all this is androstenol, a pheromone men secrete in their sweat. Women are attracted to this pheromone while most men are repelled by it. So perhaps women knit men extra-warm sweaters subconciously hoping to get a whiff of this pheromone. And maybe men agree to wear these sweaters, despite their overactive sweat glands, because it helps them attract more women. And maybe, just maybe, that explains the

Yarns to Keep Him Cool

- Yarns made from cellulose fibers, such as cotton, hemp, and linen, are ideal for men who overheat since these fibers actually pull heat away from the body. Unmercerized cotton is especially suited for men as it has a matte finish (unlike the natural sheen of hemp and linen). Bear in mind, though, that cellulose fibers can be dense and heavy, so avoid bulky cotton yarns and elaborate yarn-gobbling stitchwork or else you'll have a weight issue with which to contend.

- Though some may think that wool is too hot for men to wear, wool actually has an amazing ability to absorb and release moisture, which prevents heat and moisture from being trapped against the wearer's body. Yarns like this are often referred to as "breathable." Merino wool is amongst the softest and most breathable yarns available.

- Blends made from cotton and wool combine the best of both worlds: Cotton allows air to circulate between his skin and the outside world, while wool, which is naturally more lightweight and elastic, adds a bit of stretch and structure and will keep the garment from getting too heavy.

- Pure cashmere is eight times warmer than wool, so it is likely to be too hot for most guys if used on its own. Instead, look for a blend that contains a small amount of cashmere for a little softness and warmth, along with a breathable fiber like cotton or merino.

- Although not as warm as cashmere, alpaca is still several times warmer than wool. If you simply love working with alpaca, try using it in a blend when knitting for your man.

- Synthetic fibers do not breathe like wool and cellulose fibers, so a sweater made from them can be uncomfortable for people who easily overheat. Consider synthetic-natural fiber blends as an alternative.

so-called "boyfriend curse"—that's when a man breaks up with his girlfriend as soon as she knits him a sweater. That warmth gets his androstenol flowing and soon other women are flocking to him like moths to a flame.

All of this is to say that if you're a knitter wanting to make a sweater for a guy with a sweat issue, take time to choose your yarn wisely. If he is the type of guy who sweats at the mere thought of dinner with your parents, a lightweight cotton may be in order. For a guy who doesn't overheat too easily, a blend of wool and another fiber that doesn't trap heat, such as cotton or linen, would be a good choice. And any man, no matter how much he sweats, has an appreciation for cardigans since he can always wear them open and let the air rush in—all in a civilized, non-"Hulk"-like fashion.

BASIC **CARDIGAN** TWO WAYS

Here's a tailored cardigan in two casual styles: one with buttons in a lightweight wool blend, and the other with a zipper in a cotton yarn. The pattern is simple butclassic, with wide vertical stripes created from alternating bands of stockinette stitch and reverse stockinette stitch. The shoulders are tailored to sit up high, bringing the sleeves with them. Check the measurements on the schematic against your guy's arm measurements, then adjust the length if necessary.

Sizes	Small (Medium, Large, X-Large, 2X-Large, 3X-Large)
Finished Measurements	40 (44, 48, 52, 56, 60)" chest, unblocked 41 (45, 49, 53, 57, 61)" chest, blocked flat
Notions	Button Version: six (six, seven, seven, seven, eight) ⅞" buttons Zipper Version: 24 (24, 26, 26, 26, 26)" separating zipper; sewing needle and matching thread
Stitch Pattern	**1x1 Rib** (multiple of 2 sts; 2-row repeat) **All Rows:** *K1, p1; repeat from * to end.
Notes	This pattern is customizable for multiple sizes and multiple gauges. First make a Stockinette stitch swatch with the yarn you are using to determine appropriate gauge. Then determine the finished chest measurement you want. To make it easier to follow the pattern, you might want to highlight all the numbers that pertain to your chosen gauge and size.

BUTTON CARDIGAN SHOWN ABOVE.
SIZE: Medium; **FINISHED MEASUREMENTS:** 44" chest; **YARN:** Classic Elite Yarns Portland Tweed (50% virgin wool / 25% alpaca / 25% viscose; 120 yards / 50 grams): 11 balls #5038 Major Brown; **NEEDLES:** One pair straight needles size US 7 (4.5 mm), one 16" (40 cm) long circular (circ) needle size US 7 (4.5 mm). Change needle size if necessary to obtain correct gauge. **GAUGE:** 18 sts and 26 rows = 4" (10 cm) in Stockinette stitch (St st)

Yarn Requirements

		FINISHED CHEST MEASUREMENT					
		40	**44**	**48**	**52**	**56**	**60"**
Button Version	3½	1070	1165	1285	1365	1475	1550 yards
GAUGE	4	1185	1275	1415	1495	1620	1710
	4½	1285	1400	1545	1640	1780	1875
	5	1415	1520	1675	1775	1935	2035
Zipper Version	3½	1025	1115	1235	1315	1420	1500 yards
GAUGE	4	1145	1235	1370	1455	1575	1665
	4½	1240	1355	1500	1595	1730	1825
	5	1365	1470	1620	1720	1880	1980

Back

CO

3½	74	82	88	96	102	110 sts.
4	84	92	100	108	116	124
4½	94	104	112	122	130	140
5	104	114	124	134	144	154

Begin Pattern (RS): NOTE: *Back is worked in 5 panels, A, B, C, D, and E. Panels A, C, and E are worked in St st, and Panels B and D are worked in Rev St st.* Work Panel A in St st across the following sts:

3½	16	17	17	18	21	22 sts;
4	18	19	20	21	22	26
4½	20	22	23	25	26	28
5	22	24	26	28	30	32

work Panel B in Rev St st, C in St st, then D in Rev St st across the following sts:

3½	14	16	18	20	20	22 sts;
4	16	18	20	22	24	24
4½	18	20	22	24	26	28
5	20	22	24	26	28	30

then work Panel E in St st across the following sts:

3½	16	17	17	18	21	22 sts.
4	18	19	20	21	22	26
4½	20	22	23	25	26	28
5	22	24	26	28	30	32

Work even until piece measures 15 (15, 15½, 15½, 16, 16)" from the beginning, ending with a WS row.

SHAPE ARMHOLE

Next row (RS): At beginning of next 2 rows, BO

3½	3	4	6	7	9	9 sts.
4	4	4	7	8	10	11
4½	4	5	8	9	11	12
5	4	6	9	10	12	13

Next Row (RS): BO 2 sts at beginning of row

3½	2	2	2	4	4	8 times.
4	2	2	2	4	6	6
4½	2	2	2	4	4	8
5	2	2	2	4	6	8

	40	44	48	52	56	60"

Decrease Row (RS): K1, k2tog, work to last 3 sts, ssk, k1. Work even for 1 row.

Repeat Decrease Row every other row

GAUGE	40	44	48	52	56	60"
3½	5	6	6	6	7	7 times.
4	5	7	7	7	7	9
4½	7	8	8	9	11	10
5	8	8	9	9	10	12

Remaining sts:

GAUGE	40	44	48	52	56	60"
3½	52	56	58	60	60	60 sts.
4	60	64	66	68	68	70
4½	66	72	74	76	76	78
5	74	80	82	86	86	86

Work even until armhole measures 9½ (9½, 10, 10, 10½, 10½)", ending with a WS row.

SHAPE SHOULDERS AND NECK

Next Row (RS): At beginning of next 4 rows, BO

GAUGE	40	44	48	52	56	60"
3½	4	5	5	5	5	5 sts,
4	4	5	5	5	5	6
4½	5	6	6	6	6	6
5	5	6	6	7	7	7

then at beginning of next 2 rows, BO

GAUGE	40	44	48	52	56	60"
3½	3	3	3	4	4	4 sts.
4	5	5	5	6	6	5
4½	4	5	5	6	6	7
5	6	7	6	6	6	6

BO remaining sts each shoulder:

GAUGE	40	44	48	52	56	60"
3½	30	30	32	32	32	32 sts.
4	34	34	36	36	36	36
4½	38	38	40	40	40	40
5	42	42	46	46	46	46

Right Front
Button Version

CO

GAUGE	40	44	48	52	56	60"
3½	41	45	48	52	55	59 sts.
4	47	51	55	59	63	67
4½	52	56	61	65	70	74
5	56	61	66	71	76	81

Begin Pattern (RS): NOTE: *Right Front is worked in 4 panels, A, B, C, and D. Panel A, the buttonhole band, is worked in 1x1 Rib, Panels B and D are worked in Rev St st, and Panel C is worked in St st.* Work Panel A in 1x1 Rib across 8 sts; work Panel B in Rev St st across the following sts:

GAUGE	40	44	48	52	56	60"
3½	3	4	5	6	6	7 sts;
4	5	6	7	8	9	9
4½	6	6	8	8	10	10
5	6	7	8	9	10	11

FINISHED CHEST MEASUREMENT					
40	**44**	**48**	**52**	**56**	**60"**

work Panel C in St st across the following sts:

GAUGE

	40	44	48	52	56	60"
3½	14	16	18	20	20	22 sts;
4	16	18	20	22	24	24
4½	18	20	22	24	26	28
5	20	22	24	26	28	30

then work Panel D in Rev St st across the following sts:

GAUGE

	40	44	48	52	56	60"
3½	16	17	17	18	21	22 sts.
4	18	19	20	21	22	26
4½	20	22	23	25	26	28
5	22	24	26	28	30	32

Work even until armhole measures 6 (6, 6½, 6½, 7, 7)", working armhole shaping as for Back, ending with a WS row.

Remaining sts:

GAUGE

	40	44	48	52	56	60"
3½	30	32	33	34	34	34 sts.
4	35	37	38	39	39	40
4½	38	40	42	42	43	43
5	41	44	45	47	47	47

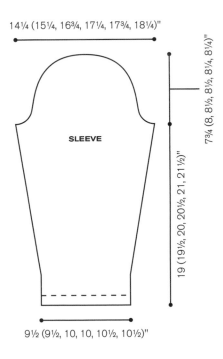

SLEEVE

14¼ (15¼, 16¾, 17¼, 17¾, 18¼)"

7¾ (8, 8½, 8½, 8¼, 8¼)"

19 (19½, 20, 20½, 21, 21½)"

9½ (9½, 10, 10, 10½, 10½)"

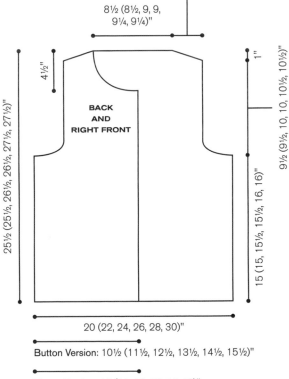

BACK AND RIGHT FRONT

3¼ (3¾, 3¾, 4, 4, 4)"

8½ (8½, 9, 9, 9¼, 9¼)"

4½"

1"

9½ (9½, 10, 10, 10½, 10½)"

25½ (25½, 26½, 26½, 27½, 27½)"

15 (15, 15½, 15½, 16, 16)"

20 (22, 24, 26, 28, 30)"

Button Version: 10½ (11½, 12½, 13½, 14½, 15½)"

Zipper Version: 10 (11, 12, 13, 14, 15)"

	40	44	48	52	56	60"

SHAPE NECK

Next Row (RS): BO

GAUGE	40	44	48	52	56	60"
3½	14	15	16	17	17	17 sts, work to end.
4	15	16	17	18	18	18
4½	16	17	18	19	19	19
5	17	18	19	20	20	20

Work even for 1 row.

Next Row (RS): BO 2 sts at neck edge every other row

GAUGE	40	44	48	52	56	60"
3½	2	2	2	1	1	1 time(s).
4	3	2	2	1	1	1
4½	2	2	2	1	1	1
5	3	3	4	3	3	3

Work even for 1 row.

Next Row (RS): Decrease 1 st at neck edge every other row

GAUGE	40	44	48	52	56	60"
3½	1	0	0	1	1	1 time(s).
4	1	2	2	3	3	3
4½	4	2	3	3	4	3
5	2	1	0	1	1	1

Remaining sts:

GAUGE	40	44	48	52	56	60"
3½	11	13	13	14	14	14 sts.
4	13	15	15	16	16	17
4½	14	17	17	18	18	19
5	16	19	18	20	20	20

Work even until armhole measures same as for Back to shoulder shaping; shape shoulder as for Back.

Right Front
Zipper Version

CO

GAUGE	40	44	48	52	56	60"
3½	37	41	44	48	51	55 sts.
4	42	46	50	54	58	62
4½	47	52	56	61	65	70
5	52	57	62	67	72	77

Begin Pattern (RS): NOTE: *Right Front is worked in 3 panels, A, B, and C. Panels A and C are worked in Rev St st, and Panel B is worked in St st.* Work Panel A in Rev St st across the following sts:

GAUGE	40	44	48	52	56	60"
3½	7	8	9	10	10	11 sts;
4	8	9	10	11	12	12
4½	9	10	11	12	13	14
5	10	11	12	13	14	15

work Panel B in St st across the following sts:

GAUGE	40	44	48	52	56	60"
3½	14	16	18	20	20	22 sts;
4	16	18	20	22	24	24
4½	18	20	22	24	26	28
5	20	22	24	26	28	30

then work Panel C in Rev St st across the following sts:

GAUGE	40	44	48	52	56	60"
3½	16	17	17	18	21	22 sts.
4	18	19	20	21	22	26
4½	20	22	23	25	26	28
5	22	24	26	28	30	32

GAUGE	40	44	48	52	56	60"

Work even until armhole measures 6 (6, 6½, 6½, 7, 7)", working armhole shaping as for Back, ending with a WS row.

Remaining sts:

GAUGE	40	44	48	52	56	60"
3½	26	28	29	30	30	30 sts.
4	30	32	33	34	34	35
4½	33	36	37	38	38	39
5	37	40	41	43	43	43

SHAPE NECK

Next Row (RS): BO

GAUGE	40	44	48	52	56	60"
3½	6	7	8	9	9	9 sts, work to end.
4	7	8	9	10	10	10
4½	8	9	10	11	11	11
5	9	10	11	12	12	12

Work even for 1 row.

Next Row (RS): BO 2 sts at neck edge every other row

GAUGE	40	44	48	52	56	60"
3½	2	2	2	1	1	1 time(s).
4	3	2	2	1	1	1
4½	2	2	2	1	1	1
5	3	3	4	3	3	3

Work even for 1 row.

Next Row (RS): Decrease 1 st at neck edge every other row

GAUGE	40	44	48	52	56	60"
3½	5	4	4	5	5	5 times.
4	4	5	5	6	6	6
4½	7	6	6	7	7	7
5	6	5	4	5	5	5

Remaining sts:

GAUGE	40	44	48	52	56	60"
3½	11	13	13	14	14	14 sts.
4	13	15	15	16	16	17
4½	14	17	17	18	18	19
5	16	19	18	20	20	20

Work even until armhole measures same as for Back to shoulder shaping; shape shoulder as for Back.

Left Front

Button Version

Place markers for buttons on Right Front, the first 4 rows from the bottom edge, the last 1" from the top edge, and the remaining 4 (4, 5, 5, 5, 6) evenly spaced between. Work as for Right Front, reversing all shaping, reversing order of Panels A-D, and working Manly Buttonholes (see facing page) opposite markers.

Zipper Version

Work as for Right Front, reversing all shaping and reversing order of Panels A-C.

Sleeves

CO

GAUGE	40	44	48	52	56	60"
3½	32	32	34	34	36	36 sts.
4	38	38	40	40	42	42
4½	42	42	44	44	46	46
5	46	46	48	48	52	52

Men aren't dainty. Therefore, they need manly buttonholes, which are stronger than standard buttonholes and able to withstand some bullish abuse. This method gives extra strength at the edges to hold up to years of rough handling.

Note that these buttonholes are designed for ⅞" buttons. If your buttonholes appear to be too small, repeat Step 3 three times instead of twice when working Step 4. If you are using buttons smaller than ⅞" you may want to make the holes smaller by skipping Step 3. Buttons larger than ⅞" are too feminine for most men.

Step 1: Working on a WS row, k1, p1, k1, slip 1 wyif, bring yarn to back.
Step 2: Slip 1 wyib, pass first slipped stitch over second slipped stitch.
Step 3: Slip 1 wyib, pass stitch over.
Step 4: Repeat Step 3 twice, then slip last stitch back to left-hand needle, turn.
Step 5: Bring yarn to back, cast on 5 sts using Cable CO method (see Special Techniques, page 122), turn.
Step 6: Leaving yarn at back, slip first stitch from left-hand needle to right-hand needle, pass last cast-on stitch over slipped stitch.
Work the rest of your row.

Begin St st, beginning with a knit row. Work even for 1", ending with a WS row. Purl 1 row (turning row). Continuing in St st, work even until piece measures 2" from turning row, ending with a WS row.

	FINISHED CHEST MEASUREMENT					
	40	**44**	**48**	**52**	**56**	**60"**
SHAPE SLEEVE	**Next Row (RS):** Increase 1 st each side this row, every 8 (8, 6, 6, 6, 6) rows					
3½	7	2	11	11	12	12 time(s),
4	9	4	13	13	14	14
4½	10	6	14	14	15	16
5	9	5	16	16	1	17
	then every 6 (6, 4, 4, 4, 4) rows					
3½	1	8	0	1	0	1 time(s).
4	0	7	0	1	0	1
4½	0	6	1	2	1	1
5	3	9	1	2	16	2
	Total sts:					
3½	50	54	58	60	62	64 sts.
4	58	62	68	70	72	74
4½	64	68	76	78	80	82
5	72	76	84	86	88	92

Work even until piece measures 18 (18½, 19, 19½, 20, 20½)" from turning row, ending with a WS row.

	FINISHED CHEST MEASUREMENT					
	40	44	48	52	56	60"

SHAPE CAP

Next Row (RS): At beginning of next 2 rows, BO

GAUGE	40	44	48	52	56	60"
3½	2	3	5	6	8	8 sts.
4	3	3	6	7	9	10
4½	3	4	7	8	10	11
5	3	5	8	9	11	12

Decrease Row (RS): K1, ssk, knit to last 3 sts, k2tog, k1. Work even for 1 row.

Repeat Decrease Row every other row

GAUGE	40	44	48	52	56	60"
3½	18	19	20	20	19	19 times.
4	19	22	23	23	22	22
4½	23	24	26	26	25	25
5	26	27	29	29	28	28

Work even for 1 row. BO remaining

GAUGE	40	44	48	52	56	60"
3½	8	8	6	6	6	6 sts.
4	12	10	8	8	8	8
4½	10	10	8	8	8	8
5	12	12	8	8	8	8

Finishing

Sew shoulder seams. Set in Sleeves. Fold Sleeve hem to WS at turning row and sew to WS, being careful not to let sts show on RS. Sew side and Sleeve seams.

COLLAR

With RS facing, using circular needle, beginning 4 sts in from Front edge for Button Version and at Front edge for Zipper Version, working along neck shaping, pick up and knit:

	40	44	48	52	56	60"
3½	75	77	81	87	87	87 sts.
4	85	89	93	99	99	99
4½	99	101	105	111	111	111
5	109	111	115	123	123	123

Next Row (WS): Begin 1x1 Rib, beginning and ending with p1. Work even until piece measures 5 (5, 5½, 5½, 6, 6)" from pick-up row. BO all sts in pattern.

Button Version

Fold Collar over to WS and sew to pick-up row. Sew side edges of Collar closed. Sew buttons opposite buttonholes.

Zipper Version

Using sewing needle and matching thread, sew zipper to Fronts, beginning at bottom edge. Trim excess zipper at top edge if necessary, folding Collar over top of zipper to WS. Sew zipper to both side edges of Collar. Sew BO edge of Collar to pick-up row.

ZIPPER CARDIGAN SHOWN AT RIGHT.

SIZE: Large; **FINISHED MEASUREMENTS**: 48" chest; **YARN**: Rowan Yarns Cotton Jeans (100% cotton; 82 yards / 50 grams): 17 balls #366 Blue Jeans; **NEEDLES**: One pair straight needles size US 7 (4.5 mm), one 16" (40 cm) long circular (circ) needle size US 7 (4.5 mm). Change needle size if necessary to obtain correct gauge. **GAUGE**: 18 sts and 26 rows = 4" (10 cm) in Stockinette stitch (St st)

Men **Hate** Fittings

RAGLAN-SLEEVED **HENLEY**

Men and women behave differently; we all know it's true. In general, women cry and men don't. Women share their feelings, men don't. And women try on clothes, while men don't. According to Federated Department Stores' website, women try on clothes 10 times more often than men do. Most men won't even go into the fitting room when they buy a pair of jeans. They simply choose a pair because the label tells them it's their size or it's the same size they bought last time. And in the rare event that a man does try on a piece of clothing, he certainly won't step out of the dressing room to show his friends.

On the other hand, women would like everything to fit perfectly and they'll go to extremes to make it happen. My sister had six fittings for her wedding dress before she claimed it fit right, and she had my mother and her friends join her each time just to make sure.

Men aren't willing to put in that kind of effort. The first time a man tries on a new shirt is most likely the first time he puts it on to wear it. And if it doesn't fit, he might just wear it anyway (see Rule #9: Men Are Oblivious; page 108). If anyone notices, he'll blame the manufacturer. In the case of a handmade sweater, however, that manufacturer is you. Would your guy actually blame you if the sweater you made him didn't fit perfectly? Not if he knows what's good for him. But you want it to fit right, which means he'll need to let you take some measurements before you start—and he may even need to try it on.

There are a couple of ways to go about getting his measurements. You could catch him in a good mood or when he owes you a favor—perhaps the day after he forgot your anniversary, or a week before his mother comes for a visit. When you have that chance, take all of his measurements to keep on hand for the future (see the chart at right); these will stand you in good stead as long as he doesn't gain or lose a lot of weight or bulk up at the gym. You could also use the technique my grandmother always used with me: Find a sweater that he owns that fits well in the same style that you plan to make and take measurements off of that. Ideally, he'll also try on the sweater you're making as you go, though this can sometimes take some convincing. Here are a few tricks:

- Tell him when you start the project that you're going to need him to try on the garment three times: Once to check the chest size (if you're knitting in the round); once for the sleeve length; and finally for the length of the body. If he knows it's coming he won't be caught off guard and you've got a better chance of getting him to agree.
- Never ask him while he's watching TV, reading the paper, or engaged in some other activity that's important to him. Instead, ask him to try on the sweater in the morning as he's getting dressed or in the evening as he's getting ready for bed. With his clothes off already, he may be more willing.
- Bribe him. If you're dealing with a romantic partner, tell him you'll take something off for every piece he puts on.

Size Matters

Take your guy's measurements using a fabric measuring tape. For accuracy, measure him against his skin or with a T-shirt on. Don't pull the tape measure tight; just skim his body with it. For most men, you will want to choose a size that allows between 2 and 4 inches of ease, depending on how close- or loose-fitting he likes his clothes.

Fill in the chart, using one column for each guy for whom you're likely to knit a sweater.

NAME:				
Chest Size: Measure just under his armpits, around the fullest part of his chest and shoulder blades.				
Length: Measure from the prominent bone at the back of his neck to just above the pockets of his pants. Or, ask him to put on a sweater he likes to see where the bottom of that sweater hits his pants and then measure to the same place.				
Crossback: Measure the distance between the top bump of each shoulder. This measurement will help in fitting him for set-in sleeves.				
Sleeve Length: Measure from his armpit to where his hand meets his wrist, just past his wrist bone.				
Upper Arm Diameter: Measure around the widest part of his biceps/triceps area.				
Wrist Diameter: Measure around his wrist where it meets his hand.				
Armhole Depth: Measure from the top outside edge of his shoulder down to his armpit.				

RAGLAN-SLEEVED **HENLEY**

This simple raglan-sleeved pullover looks good on just about everyone and it's easy to get the fit just right since it's worked in the round from the top down. If he's willing to cooperate, just slip it on him while you're making it to get an instant read on the length of body and sleeves. The body is meant to reach just past his pants pockets and the sleeves are meant to reach the bottom of his palm, though of course, you can change those lengths if he prefers something different.

Sizes	Small (Medium, Large, X-Large, 2X-Large, 3X-Large)
Finished Measurements	40 (44, 48, 52, 56, 60)" chest
Notions	Stitch markers; waste yarn; six ⅝" buttons
Notes	This sweater is worked from the top down.
	This pattern is customizable for multiple sizes and multiple gauges. First make a Stockinette stitch swatch with the yarn you are using to determine appropriate gauge. Since this pattern is worked flat and in the round, it can be helpful to test your gauge both ways for accuracy (see Special Techniques, page 122). Then determine the finished chest measurement you want. To make it easier to follow the pattern, you might want to highlight all the numbers that pertain to your chosen gauge and size.

SWEATER SHOWN ABOVE.
SIZE: Medium; **FINISHED MEASUREMENTS**: 44" chest; **YARN**: Plymouth Yarn Royal Llama Silk (60% llama / 40% silk; 102 yards / 50 grams): 15 balls #1002; **NEEDLES**: One 36" (90 cm) long circular (circ) needle size US 7 (4.5 mm), one 16" (40 cm) long circular needle size US 7 (4.5 mm), one set of five double-pointed needles (dpn) size US 7 (4.5 mm). Change needle size if necessary to obtain correct gauge. **GAUGE**: 18 sts and 27 rows = 4" (10 cm) in Stockinette stitch (St st)

Yarn Requirements

	F I N I S H E D C H E S T M E A S U R E M E N T					
	40	**44**	**48**	**52**	**56**	**60"**
4	1320	1440	1610	1675	1780	1865 yards
4½	1445	1580	1760	1845	1950	2060
5	1585	1715	1930	1980	2115	2215
5½	1705	1875	2070	2170	2295	2435
6	1830	1995	2235	2325	2475	2590

(Gauge)

Yoke

NOTE: *Piece is worked from the top down.*

Using 36" long circ needle, CO 2 sts for Front, place marker (pm),

4	16 sts (all sizes) for Sleeve, pm,					
4½	18					
5	20					
5½	22					
6	24					

CO:

4	22	22	22	24	24	24 sts for Back, pm,
4½	26	26	26	28	28	28
5	28	28	28	32	32	32
5½	32	32	32	34	34	34
6	36	36	36	38	38	38

CO:

4	16 sts (all sizes) for Sleeve, pm,					
4½	18					
5	20					
5½	22					
6	24					

then CO 2 sts for Front. Total sts:

4	58	58	58	60	60	60 sts.
4½	66	66	66	68	68	68
5	72	72	72	76	76	76
5½	80	80	80	82	82	82
6	88	88	88	90	90	90

SHAPE RAGLAN

Increase Row (RS): Begin St st. K1-f/b, [knit to 1 st before marker, k1-f/b, slip marker (sm), k1-f/b] 4 times, knit to last st, k1-f/b. Work even for 1 row.

Repeat Increase Row every other row

4	4	4	4	3	3	3 times.
4½	4	4	4	4	4	4
5	4	4	5	4	4	4
5½	4	5	4	5	5	5
6	4	5	5	5	4	5

GAUGE	40	44	48	52	56	60"
Total sts:						
4	108	108	108	100	100	100 sts.
4½	116	116	116	118	118	118
5	122	122	132	126	126	126
5½	130	140	130	142	142	142
6	138	148	148	150	140	150

Work even for 1 row.

SHAPE NECK

Next Row (RS): Continue working increases before and after each marker every other row and, AT THE SAME TIME, CO 2 sts each neck edge

GAUGE	40	44	48	52	56	60"
4	0	0	0	1	1	1 time(s),
4½	1	1	1	0	0	0
5	0	0	1	1	1	1
5½	1	2	1	1	1	1
6	2	3	0	2	1	2

CO 3 sts each neck edge

GAUGE	40	44	48	52	56	60"
4	0	0	0	0	0	0 time(s),
4½	0	0	0	1	1	1
5	1	1	0	1	1	1
5½	1	0	1	1	1	1
6	1	0	2	1	2	1

then CO 8 sts each neck edge once. Total sts:

GAUGE	40	44	48	52	56	60"
4	132	132	132	136	136	136 sts.
4½	152	152	152	156	156	156
5	160	160	168	176	176	176
5½	180	188	180	192	192	192
6	200	208	200	212	204	212

Begin Placket (RS): [K1, p1] 4 times, work to last 8 sts, working raglan shaping as established, [p1, k1] 4 times. Work even for 1 row, working [p1, k1] 4 times across first 8 sts of row, and [k1, p1] across last 8 sts of row.

NOTE: *Raglan, placket, and armhole shaping will all be worked at the same time. Please read entire section through before beginning.*

SHAPE PLACKET

NOTE: *Placket shaping is worked at the same time as raglan shaping.*

Buttonhole Row (RS): K1, p1, k1, yo, k2tog, work to end, continuing to work raglan shaping as established. Work even for 1 row. Continuing raglan shaping, work 5 more buttonholes, spaced 1½" apart. After completing final buttonhole, work even for 1 row.

Join Fronts (RS): Continuing with raglan shaping, work to last 8 sts, place these sts on dpn and hold to back of work, join for working in the rnd, [k2tog (1 st from left-hand needle together with 1 st from dpn)] 8 times, work to next marker. This will be the beginning of rnd marker. AT THE SAME TIME, continue working raglan shaping.

CONTINUE RAGLAN SHAPING

NOTE: *Raglan shaping is worked at the same time as Placket shaping.*

(RS) Continuing with placket, continue to work raglan shaping as established, until you have worked a total of

GAUGE	40	44	48	52	56	60"
4	23	21	22	18	13	8 raglan increases
4½	28	24	26	20	15	10
5	30	28	27	26	18	11
5½	34	30	32	26	19	13
6	37	35	37	29	22	14

from the beginning. Work even for 1 row.

Next Row (RS): Continuing to work raglan shaping on Front and Back every other row, work raglan shaping on Sleeves every 4 rows, until you have worked an additional

GAUGE	40	44	48	52	56	60"
4	1	3	4	6	9	12 Sleeve increase(s).
4½	0	3	4	7	10	13
5	1	3	5	6	10	14
5½	0	4	5	8	12	16
6	0	3	4	0	12	17

Total sts:

GAUGE	40	44	48	52	56	60"
4	272	280	300	296	292	288 sts.
4½	312	316	344	336	332	328
5	348	356	372	384	368	360
5½	380	396	424	416	408	408
6	416	436	464	452	444	440

NOTE: *You may not complete the placket and join Fronts until after dividing for Body. If that is the case, you will have 8 more sts than the st counts given above because you have not yet worked the placket sides together.*

Work even for 1 row.

DIVIDE FOR BODY

NOTE: *If you have not yet completed the placket, continue to work back and forth while dividing for Body. You will need to work across the Left Front to the first Sleeve marker before placing the Left Sleeve sts on waste yarn, and you will work to the end of the Right Front rather than to the beginning of the rnd once you have placed the Right Sleeve sts on waste yarn.*

Place the following sts on waste yarn for Left Sleeve, removing markers:

GAUGE	40	44	48	52	56	60"
4	64	64	68	64	60	56 sts.
4½	74	72	78	72	68	64
5	82	82	84	84	76	70
5½	90	90	96	90	84	80
6	98	100	106	98	92	86

CO the following sts for left underarm, placing marker at center of CO sts for beginning of rnd:

GAUGE	40	44	48	52	56	60"
4	8	12	14	20	26	32 sts.
4½	8	14	14	22	28	36
5	8	14	18	22	32	40
5½	10	14	16	26	34	42
6	10	14	18	28	38	46

	40	44	48	52	56	60"

Work across the following sts for Back:

GAUGE

	40	44	48	52	56	60"
4	72	76	82	84	86	88 sts.
4½	82	86	94	96	98	100
5	92	96	102	108	108	110
5½	100	108	116	118	120	124
6	110	118	126	128	130	134

Place Right Sleeve sts on waste yarn. CO the same number of sts for right underarm as for left, placing marker at center of CO sts for right side. Work across Front sts; this should be the same number as for Back, unless you have not yet joined the placket sts, in which case you will have 8 additional sts across the Fronts than across the Back.

Remaining sts:

GAUGE

	40	44	48	52	56	60"
4	160	176	192	208	224	240 sts.
4½	180	200	216	236	252	272
5	200	220	240	260	280	300
5½	220	244	264	288	308	332
6	240	264	288	312	336	360

Next Rnd: Continue in St st (knit every rnd) until piece measures 16½ (16½, 17, 17, 17½, 17½)" from underarm, joining Fronts when placket is finished if you have not already done so.

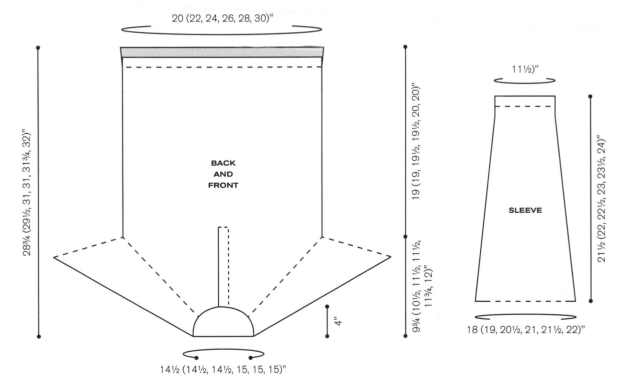

20 (22, 24, 26, 28, 30)"

BACK
AND
FRONT

28¾ (29½, 31, 31, 31¾, 32)"

19 (19, 19½, 19½, 20, 20)"

9¾ (10½, 11½, 11½, 11¾, 12)"

4"

14½ (14½, 14½, 15, 15, 15)"

11½"

SLEEVE

21½ (22, 22½, 23, 23½, 24)"

18 (19, 20½, 21, 21½, 22)"

SHAPE SLIT

Next Row (RS): Work to side marker, turn. Working back and forth on Back sts only, work even for 1½", ending with a RS row. Knit 1 row (turning row). Continue in St st for 1" from turning row. BO all sts.

Next Row (RS): Rejoin yarn to Front sts. Working back and forth, work even for 1", ending with a RS row. Knit 1 row (turning row). Continue in St st for 1" from turning row. BO all sts.

Sleeves

FINISHED CHEST MEASUREMENT					
40	44	48	52	56	60"

Transfer Sleeve sts from waste yarn to 16" circ needle. With RS facing, join yarn at underarm; work to end, pick up and knit the following sts for underarm from CO sts, placing marker at center of picked-up sts for beginning of rnd:

GAUGE

	40	44	48	52	56	60"
4	4	8	12	14	20	26	32 sts.
4½	8	14	14	22	28	36
5	8	14	18	22	32	40
5½	10	14	16	26	34	42
6	10	14	18	28	38	46

Total sts:

GAUGE

	40	44	48	52	56	60"
4	72	76	82	84	86	88 sts.
4½	82	86	92	94	96	100
5	90	96	102	106	108	110
5½	100	104	112	116	118	122
6	108	114	124	126	130	132

Begin St st; work even until piece measures 1" from pick-up rnd.

SHAPE SLEEVE

Decrease Rnd: K2tog, knit to last 2 sts, ssk. NOTE: *Change to dpns when necessary for number of sts on needle.*

Repeat Decrease Rnd every 7 rnds

GAUGE

	40	44	48	52	56	60"
4	12	12	4	3	1	0 time(s),
4½	14	10	3	1	0	0
5	16	11	4	0	0	0
5½	18	15	5	1	1	0
6	19	16	4	3	0	0

then every 5 rnds

GAUGE

	40	44	48	52	56	60"
4	0	2	13	15	18	20 time(s).
4½	1	7	17	20	22	24
5	0	8	18	24	25	26
5½	0	5	19	25	26	29
6	0	6	23	25	30	31

Remaining sts:

GAUGE

4	46 sts (all sizes).
4½	50
5	56
5½	62
6	68

Work even until piece measures 20½ (21, 21½, 22, 22½, 23)" from pick-up rnd. Purl 1 rnd (turning rnd). Work even for 1" from turning rnd. BO all sts. Fold hem to WS at turning rnd and sew to WS, being careful not to let sts shown on RS.

Finishing

NECKBAND

FINISHED CHEST MEASUREMENT					
40	**44**	**48**	**52**	**56**	**60"**

With RS facing, using 16" circ needle, beginning at center neck edge, working along neck shaping, pick up and knit:

4	84	84	84	86	86	86 sts.
4½	96	96	96	100	100	100
5	104	104	104	112	112	112
5½	116	116	116	120	120	120
6	128	128	128	132	132	132

Next Row (WS): Purl 1 row. Knit 1 row. Knit 1 row (turning row). Knit 1 row. Purl 1 row. BO all sts. Fold Neckband to WS at turning row and sew to WS at pick-up row. Sew side edges of Neckband.

Fold Body and Sleeve hems to WS at turning row and sew to WS, being careful not to let sts show on RS. Sew side edges of Body hem. Sew buttons opposite buttonholes. Block as desired.

Not **All** Men Are **Worthy** **of** Cashmere

HOODED **SWEATSHIRT**

As knitters, we put a lot of effort into our projects. From the money we spend on yarn to the sheer number of hours it takes us to finish what we start, it's no surprise that so much of our ego gets knitted into our creations. It's easy to believe that everyone around us should appreciate the value of what we make, but the truth is that most non-knitters, which accounts for most of the men in our lives, won't. Our husbands, boyfriends, and sons may be *happy* that we found something we enjoy, but they may never understand the subtle beauty of the stitches or fully grasp the time and effort that goes into the process. And so it takes an enormous amount of patience and forgiveness on our part when they lose, abuse, neglect, give away, or otherwise compromise a garment we've made with our own two hands.

So, before you start knitting for any man, you need to take off your rose-colored glasses and take a cold, hard look at who he is. If he is careful and meticulous about everything, you're cleared to knit him whatever he likes—no matter what it costs or how much time it takes.

But if he's on the careless side, especially when it comes to clothing, proceed with caution. Prepare for the worst he can do and select materials based on the toughest treatment the project, your ego, and your relationship can withstand.

Consider this story from Jenna of Akron, Ohio. (Warning: it's a little gross.)

Jenna's husband had begged her to make him a soft hat. While she could have gone for something practical—strong, inexpensive, and washable—she let her husband pick out the yarn: fingering-weight black cashmere. She knitted it quickly and presented it to him on a Saturday morning right after breakfast.

"Was he pleased?" I asked. And here comes the gross part, in Jenna's words:

"Three hours after he received it—picture if you will—one of our cats begins to make *that* sound (coupled with some horrid body jerks) and yucks up onto the floor. Dear husband reaches *past* the roll of paper towels conveniently at hand, bypasses the Kleenex, moves *around* the dirty T-shirt he had left on the floor, and casually swipes up the mess with the hat."

When her shrieks of horror faded, Jenna's husband looked at her, looked down, and then shrugged.

"What? No big deal to wash it, right?" he asked, not realizing that one can't just toss cashmere in the washing machine.

While Jenna's story is admittedly extreme, the truth is that many men don't show their clothes the same care they show, say, their cars, motorcycles, or golf clubs. But that doesn't mean we shouldn't knit for them. We just need to use good judgment when deciding what to knit and what type of yarn to knit it with. For instance, if your man knows enough to hand-wash his hand-knits (or to ask you to do it), he's proven he can be trusted with fine fibers like cashmere. If, on the other hand, you find him polishing the spokes of his chopper with the scarf you made him last Christmas, don't throw pearls before swine. Knit for him with inexpensive, machine-washable yarn and keep the cashmere for yourself.

Managing Mishaps

- To remove greasy food stains, soak the garment in cool water with a little baby shampoo until the solids have softened and can be dislodged with some gentle hand agitation. Drain and repeat, gently pushing the suds through the stained area. Soak for 15 minutes more, drain, then rinse. A little clear glycerin can also help—just rub it in along with the baby shampoo. To remove blood and grass stains, soak the garment with a little baking soda along with a mild detergent.

- We all know that men love to take off what they wear and throw it directly into the hamper—dirty or not. Instead of washing the whole garment, fish it out of the laundry and treat small stains with a little spot remover.

- To get wax out of a knitted garment, place plain brown paper over the area, cover with a rag and place a hot iron on top. The heat of the iron will melt the wax, which will be absorbed into the paper. Repeat with fresh paper as many times as necessary to remove as much of the wax as possible. Do not pick at the wax or you're likely to tear or pull the yarn.

- To fix a snag or a pull, turn the garment inside out and use a thin crochet hook to grab the pulled yarn and bring it to the back. Tug gently at the stitches in all directions around the pull to ease the yarn back into the pattern. If there is still a stretched-out loop in the back, use the crochet hook to twist the loop, then pull the stretched-out stitch through the twist, creating a knot on the inside of the sweater. A touch of Fray Check will keep it from coming undone.

- The biggest mistake any man can make is to lose what you knit him. For this extreme situation, keep a knitting journal with all of your notes on every project so you can remake any garment for your guy if he accidentally ruins or loses it. That is, of course, if you're willing to give him a second chance.

The same can be said about the time you spend working on the garment—don't go to the trouble of knitting him a large item like a sweater if history has proven that he is likely to ruin it. Instead, knit him a simple hat (page 114) or a pair of fingerless mitts (page 90) using stash yarn or yarn that isn't expensive. Your heart is less likely to break if he loses something small and cheap rather than something large and pricey.

If your guy falls into the gray area—he understands the value of nice clothes and has a manageable number of clothing mishaps—look for a compromise. Make him a sweater at a larger gauge that won't take months to finish, and use a machine-washable yarn that has a good blend of high-quality natural fibers and hard-working synthetic ones. He'll be happy, you'll be happy, and the relationship will remain on healthy ground.

HOODED **SWEATSHIRT**

This sweater combines the classic comfort of a simple sweatshirt with a little casual style. It's knitted up in a soft, thick blend of merino and microfiber, so even if he rolls it into a ball, uses it as a pillow, or shoves it into a drawer without folding it, the sweater will still look good when he wears it.

Sizes	Small (Medium, Large, X-Large, 2X-Large, 3X-Large)
Finished Measurements	40 (44, 48, 52, 56, 60)" chest
Notions	Stitch holders
Stitch Patterns	**1x2 Rib** (multiple of 3 sts + 2; 2-row repeat) **Row 1 (RS):** P2, *k1, p2; repeat from * to end. **Row 2:** K2, *p1, k2; repeat from * to end. Repeat Rows 1 and 2 for 1x2 Rib. **Ridge Pattern** (any number of sts; 6-row repeat) **Rows 1 (WS)-3:** Purl. **Rows 4-6:** Knit. Repeat Rows 1-6 for Ridge Pattern.
Notes	This pattern is customizable for multiple sizes and multiple gauges. First make a Stockinette stitch swatch with the yarn you are using to determine appropriate gauge. Then determine the finished chest measurement you want. To make it easier to follow the pattern, you might want to highlight all the numbers that pertain to your chosen gauge and size.

SWEATSHIRT SHOWN ABOVE.
SIZE: Medium; **FINISHED MEASUREMENTS:** 44" chest; **YARN:** GGH Aspen (50% merino / 50% acrylic microfiber; 63 yards / 50 grams): 18 balls #7 (MC); 3 balls #65 (A); **NEEDLES:** One pair straight needles size US 10 (6 mm), one 16" (40 cm) long circular (circ) needle size US 10 (6 mm). Change needle size if necessary to obtain correct gauge. **GAUGE:** 14 sts and 21 rows = 4" (10 cm) in Stockinette stitch (St st)

	FINISHED CHEST MEASUREMENT					
	40	44	48	52	56	60"
3	1060	1120	1210	1275	1375	1425 yards MC
3½	1190	1265	1370	1450	1550	1625
4	1320	1400	1525	1610	1715	1790
4½	1455	1545	1665	1760	1885	1975
5	1580	1675	1815	1915	2050	2140
3	135	150	175	190	215	230 yards A
3½	155	170	195	210	240	255
4	170	185	215	235	265	285
4½	185	205	240	260	295	315
5	200	220	260	280	320	340

(GAUGE indicated at left for each group)

Back

With MC, CO

3	56	62	68	74	80	86 sts.
3½	65	71	77	86	92	101
4	74	83	89	98	107	113
4½	83	92	101	110	119	128
5	92	101	113	122	131	143

Begin 1x2 Rib; work even until piece measures 2½ (2½, 2½, 3, 3, 3)" from the beginning, ending with a WS row, increase the following sts evenly spaced across last row:

3	4	4	4	4	4	4 sts.
3½	5	7	7	6	6	5
4	6	5	7	6	5	7
4½	7	8	7	8	7	8
5	8	9	7	8	9	7

Total sts:

3	60	66	72	78	84	90 sts.
3½	70	78	84	92	98	106
4	80	88	96	104	112	120
4½	90	100	108	118	126	136
5	100	110	120	130	140	150

Work even until piece measures 15 (15, 15½, 15½, 16, 16)" from the beginning, ending with a WS row.

Next Row (RS): Change to A. Work even until piece measures 19 (19, 19½, 19½, 20, 20)" from the beginning, ending with a WS row.

SHAPE ARMHOLES

Next Row (RS): At beginning of next 2 rows, BO

3	3	3	4	5	6	8 sts.
3½	3	4	5	7	8	9
4	4	5	6	7	9	10
4½	4	6	6	8	10	12
5	5	6	7	9	11	13

	FINISHED CHEST MEASUREMENT					
	40	**44**	**48**	**52**	**56**	**60"**

Next Row (RS): BO 2 sts at beginning of row

GAUGE

	40	44	48	52	56	60"
3	0	2	2	2	2	4 times.
3½	2	2	2	4	4	6
4	2	2	2	4	4	6
4½	2	2	2	4	4	6
5	2	2	2	4	4	6

Next Row (RS): Decrease 1 st each side this row, then every other row

GAUGE

	40	44	48	52	56	60"
3	2	1	2	3	4	3 time(s).
3½	1	2	2	2	3	3
4	1	2	3	3	4	4
4½	2	3	4	4	5	5
5	2	3	5	5	6	6

Remaining sts:

GAUGE

	40	44	48	52	56	60"
3	48	52	54	56	58	58 sts.
3½	56	60	64	64	66	68
4	64	68	72	74	76	78
4½	72	76	82	84	86	88
5	80	86	90	92	96	98

Work even until armhole measures 1½ (1½, 2, 2, 2½, 2½)", ending with a WS row. Change to MC. Work even until armhole measures 9 (9, 9½, 9½, 10, 10)", ending with a WS row.

SHAPE NECK

Next Row (RS): Work

GAUGE

	40	44	48	52	56	60"
3	19	21	22	22	23	23 sts,
3½	22	24	26	25	26	27
4	25	27	29	29	30	31
4½	29	31	34	33	34	35
5	32	35	37	36	38	39

place following sts on holder for Hood:

GAUGE

	40	44	48	52	56	60"
3	10	10	10	12	12	12 sts.
3½	12	12	12	14	14	14
4	14	14	14	16	16	16
4½	14	14	14	18	18	18
5	16	16	16	20	20	20

Join a second ball of yarn, work to end. Working both sides at the same time, BO 2 sts at each neck edge

GAUGE

	40	44	48	52	56	60"
3	1	1	1	1	1	1 time(s),
3½	1	1	1	1	1	1
4	1	1	1	1	1	1
4½	1	1	1	1	1	1
5	2	2	2	1	1	1

then decrease 1 st each neck edge every other row

GAUGE

	40	44	48	52	56	60"
3	0	0	0	0	0	0 time(s).
3½	1	1	1	1	1	1
4	1	1	1	1	1	1
4½	2	2	2	1	1	1
5	1	1	1	2	2	2

FINISHED	CHEST	MEASUREMENT			
40	44	48	52	56	60"

Work even until armhole measures 10 (10, 10½, 10½, 11, 11)", ending with a WS row. BO remaining sts each shoulder:

GAUGE

	40	44	48	52	56	60"
3	17	19	20	20	21	21 sts.
3½	19	21	23	22	23	24
4	22	24	26	26	27	28
4½	25	27	30	30	31	32
5	27	30	32	32	34	35

Front

Work as for Back until armhole measures 3 (3, 3½, 3½, 4, 4)", ending with a WS row. Remaining sts:

GAUGE

3	48	52	54	56	58	58 sts.
3½	56	60	64	64	66	68
4	64	68	72	74	76	78
4½	72	76	82	84	86	88
5	80	86	90	92	96	98

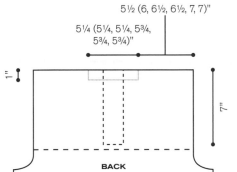

5½ (6, 6½, 6½, 7, 7)"

5¼ (5¼, 5¼, 5¾, 5¾, 5¾)"

1"

7"

10 (10, 10½, 10½, 11, 11)"

BACK AND FRONT

29 (29, 30, 30, 31, 31)"

19 (19, 19½, 19½, 20, 20)"

20 (22, 24, 26, 28, 30)"

18½ (20½, 22½, 24½, 26½, 28½)"

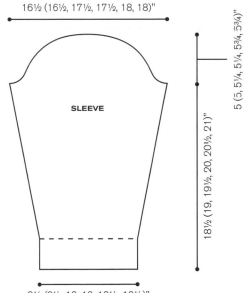

16½ (16½, 17½, 17½, 18, 18)"

5 (5, 5¼, 5¼, 5¾, 5¾)"

SLEEVE

18½ (19, 19½, 20, 20½, 21)"

9½ (9½, 10, 10, 10½, 10½)"

GAUGE	40	44	48	52	56	60"

SHAPE PLACKET

Next Row (RS): Work

GAUGE	40	44	48	52	56	60"
3	27	29	30	31	32	32 sts;
3½	31	33	35	35	36	37
4	36	38	40	41	42	43
4½	40	42	45	46	47	48
5	44	47	49	50	52	53

join a second ball of yarn, CO

GAUGE		
3	6 sts (all sizes) for right placket, work to end.
3½	6
4	8
4½	8
5	8

Next Row (WS): Working both sides at the same time, on right side, work in St st to CO sts, work in Ridge Pattern to end; on left side, work same number of sts as for right side in Ridge Pattern, work in St st to end.

Work even until armhole measures 10 (10, 10½, 10½, 11, 11)", ending with a WS row.

Next row (RS): Shape shoulders as for Back. Place remaining sts on each side on holders for Hood:

GAUGE	40	44	48	52	56	60"
3	10	10	10	11	11	11 sts.
3½	12	12	12	13	13	13
4	14	14	14	15	15	15
4½	15	15	15	16	16	16
5	17	17	17	18	18	18

Sleeves

With MC, CO

GAUGE	40	44	48	52	56	60"
3	29	29	29	29	32	32 sts.
3½	32	32	35	35	38	38
4	38	38	41	41	41	41
4½	44	44	44	44	47	47
5	47	47	50	50	53	53

Begin 1x2 Rib; work even until piece measures 3" from the beginning, ending with a WS row, increase the following sts evenly spaced across last row:

GAUGE	40	44	48	52	56	60"
3	1	1	1	1	0	0 st(s).
3½	2	2	1	1	0	0
4	2	2	1	1	3	3
4½	0	0	2	2	1	1
5	1	1	2	2	1	1

Total sts:

GAUGE	40	44	48	52	56	60"
3	30	30	30	30	32	32 sts.
3½	34	34	36	36	38	38
4	40	40	42	42	44	44
4½	44	44	46	46	48	48
5	48	48	52	52	54	54

Next Row (RS): Change to St st. Work even until piece measures 4½" from the beginning, ending with a WS row.

	40	44	48	52	56	60"

SHAPE SLEEVE

Next Row (RS): Increase 1 st each side this row, every

GAUGE

	40	44	48	52	56	60"
3	8	8	6	6	8	8 rows
3½	6	8	6	8	8	8
4	8	8	8	8	8	8
4½	6	6	6	8	8	8
5	6	6	8	8	8	8

GAUGE

	40	44	48	52	56	60"
3	1	2	9	10	3	4 time(s),
3½	11	2	12	1	3	4
4	3	4	3	4	6	7
4½	15	15	16	1	3	4
5	16	17	2	4	6	7

then every

GAUGE

	40	44	48	52	56	60"
3	6	6	4	4	6	6 rows
3½	0	6	0	6	6	6
4	6	6	6	6	6	6
4½	0	0	0	6	6	6
5	4	0	0	6	6	6

GAUGE

	40	44	48	52	56	60"
3	8	7	2	1	7	6 time(s).
3½	0	9	0	11	9	8
4	9	8	10	9	7	6
4½	0	0	0	15	13	12
5	1	0	15	13	11	10

Total sts:

GAUGE

	40	44	48	52	56	60"
3	50	50	54	54	54	54 sts.
3½	58	58	62	62	64	64
4	66	66	70	70	72	72
4½	76	76	80	80	82	82
5	84	84	88	88	90	90

Work even until piece measures 18½ (19, 19½, 20, 20½, 21)" from the beginning, ending with a WS row.

SHAPE CAP

Next Row (RS): At beginning of next 2 rows, BO

GAUGE

	40	44	48	52	56	60"
3	3	3	4	5	6	8 sts.
3½	3	4	5	7	8	9
4	4	5	6	7	9	10
4½	4	6	6	8	10	12
5	5	6	7	9	11	13

Next Row (RS): BO 2 sts at beginning of next 6 rows, then decrease 1 st each side every other row

GAUGE

	40	44	48	52	56	60"
3	2	2	3	4	7	7 times.
3½	2	3	4	6	8	9
4	4	5	6	7	10	11
4½	3	5	5	7	10	12
5	4	5	6	8	13	15

	FINISHED CHEST MEASUREMENT					
	40	**44**	**48**	**52**	**56**	**60"**

Next Row (RS): BO 2 sts at beginning of next

GAUGE	40	44	48	52	56	60"
3	8	8	8	6	2	0 rows,
3½	12	10	10	6	4	2
4	12	10	10	8	4	2
4½	18	14	16	12	8	4
5	20	18	18	14	8	4

then 4 sts at beginning of next 2 rows. BO remaining sts:

GAUGE	
3	4 sts (all sizes).
3½	4
4	6
4½	6
5	6

Finishing

Sew shoulder seams.

Hood

With RS facing, using circ needle and MC, work across sts from holder for right Front neck, continuing patterns as established, pick up and knit

GAUGE	
3	2 sts (all sizes) along right neck edge,
3½	3
4	3
4½	3
5	4

work across sts from holder for Back neck, pick up and knit

GAUGE	
3	2 sts (all sizes) along left neck edge, work to end.
3½	3
4	3
4½	3
5	4

Total sts:

GAUGE	40	44	48	52	56	60"
3	34	34	34	38	38	38 sts.
3½	42	42	42	46	46	46
4	48	48	48	52	52	52
4½	50	50	50	56	56	56
5	58	58	58	64	64	64

Work even for 1 row.

SHAPE HOOD

Next Row (RS): Continuing patterns as established, increase the following sts evenly across this row, then every other row once, working increases inside Ridge Pattern edge sts:

GAUGE	40	44	48	52	56	60"
3	13 sts.					
3½	14					
4	16	16	16	17	17	17
4½	20					
5	21					

	40	44	48	52	56	60"
Total sts:						
3	60	60	60	64	64	64 sts.
3½	70	70	70	74	74	74
4	80	80	80	86	86	86
4½	90	90	90	96	96	96
5	100	100	100	106	106	106

(GAUGE)

Work even until piece measures 13 (13½, 13½, 14, 14, 14½)" from pick-up row, ending with Row 4 of Ridge Pattern. Divide sts in half; join using Three-Needle BO, as follows: Hold sides with RSs facing each other and needles parallel, both pointing to the right. Holding both needles in left hand, using working yarn and a third needle same size or 1 size larger, insert third needle into first st on front needle, then into first st on back needle; knit these 2 sts together; *knit next st from each needle together (2 sts on right-hand needle); pass first st over second st to BO 1 st. Repeat from * until 1 st remains on third needle; cut yarn and fasten off. NOTE: *If you prefer, you may use Kitchener st to graft sts (see Special Techniques, page 122).*

Set in Sleeves. Sew side and Sleeve seams. Sew CO placket sts to base of Placket on WS, being sure not to let sts show on RS.

Men **Don't** Want Anything **Cute–** **Except** You

As a male knitter, I'm often torn between two objectives. 1: Finding something fulfilling and challenging to knit. 2: Knitting a garment simple and masculine enough for me to want to wear.

These two goals aren't mutually exclusive, but they are hard to achieve with one garment. And it's the crux of the problem many women face when knitting for their guys.

This design challenge was my inspiration for the baseball jersey pattern on page 82. Typically a baseball jersey is a raglan-sleeved affair with dark sleeves and a light-colored torso. I charged up the design by swapping a saddle shoulder for the raglan sleeves, making the knitting experience more interesting while staying within the realm of a classic man's sweater style.

Next, I asked Jodi, the store manager of my local yarn shop, if she wanted to knit the sample since she rarely has the chance to knit for men. While she is always up for a challenge, I knew I needed to sweeten the deal. I'm a cookbook author and so I always have lots of treats on hand to use as bribes when a favor is needed. In this case, the promise of homemade gefilte fish for Jodi's Passover seder sealed the deal. I would deliver the fish and she would deliver me a knitted jersey, assuming she didn't get bored halfway through it.

Things started off on shaky ground. Jodi finished both the back and front as I instructed her. Then she got to work on the sleeves.

"How about elbow patches?" she suggested.

"Yeah, that would look really cute."

I should have known right then, should have recognized the word coming out of my own mouth, but I've been teaching in a knitting store,

devoid of men, for so many years that "cute" seemed like a good idea at the time.

A week later, I packed up the finished jersey with a half dozen other garments I had made and headed into New York City for a meeting with the team working on the book. The photographer, the stylist, the book designer, and my two editors were all sitting around the conference room table waiting anxiously to see the projects I'd been describing to them for months.

Jared, the photographer, tried on each sweater. The cardigan needed the sleeves lengthened and the ski sweater needed the sleeves shortened. But when he slipped on the jersey everyone loved it as is—that is, until Jared turned around.

"Patches?" one editor said. "My husband wouldn't wear that."

"They're cute," Karen, the stylist, said.

This time that dreaded word hit me like a line drive. I was hoping to hear classic, handsome, sophisticated. Anything but cute. But here, in the middle of Manhattan, away from my suburban knitting store, I was shocked back into my male fashion mindset. I know men don't want their clothes to be cute. In fact, the only thing men want to be cute is *you*.

I asked for a pair of scissors and cut them off right then and there. The jersey was instantly transformed from cute back to handsome and masculine.

Upon my return to Connecticut, I asked Jodi if she would still find the jersey fun to knit without the ornamental patches.

"Sure," she said. "The fun part was shaping the shoulder and neck, not the patches."

I was relieved to hear that.

"Got anything else you need me to knit?"

This time, even without the promise of sweet poached fish, Jodi casted on for the Hooded Sweat- shirt on page 68. And I drove home from the shop knowing that I had reached the perfect balance—a garment that was fun for a knitter to make, that a man would be more than happy to wear.

BASEBALL **JERSEY**

Although baseball jerseys are traditionally raglan-sleeved, this saddle-shoulder version captures its essence with a little more challenge for the knitter. If your guy is the type who would go for it, make this sweater in his favorite team's colors, using the darker color for the sleeves and the lighter color for the body. But make sure to refer to Rule #1: Men Can't Fake It (page 14) before you begin, just in case you don't know him as well as you think you do.

Sizes	Small (Medium, Large, X-Large, 2X-Large, 3X-Large)
Finished Measurements	40 (44, 48, 52, 56, 60)" chest
Notions	Stitch marker
Stitch Patterns	**2x2 Rib** (multiple of 4 sts + 2; 2-row repeat) **Row 1 (WS):** P2, *k2, p2; repeat from * to end. **Row 2:** K2, *p2, k2; repeat from * to end. Repeat Rows 1 and 2 for 2x2 Rib. **2x2 Rib in-the-Rnd** (multiple of 4 sts; 1-rnd repeat) **All Rnds:** *K2, p2; repeat from * to end.
Notes	This pattern is customizable for multiple sizes and multiple gauges. First make a Stockinette stitch swatch with the yarn you are using to determine appropriate gauge. Then determine the finished chest measurement you want. To make it easier to follow the pattern, you might want to highlight all the numbers that pertain to your chosen gauge and size.

BASEBALL JERSEY SHOWN ABOVE.
SIZE: Medium; **FINISHED MEASUREMENTS:** 44" chest; **YARN:** Berroco Pure Merino (100% extrafine merino; 92 yards / 50 grams): 9 balls #8570 Storm (MC); 7 balls #8576 Coal Tar (A); **NEEDLES:** One pair straight needles size US 9 (5.5 mm); one 16" (40 cm) long circular (circ) needle size US 9 (5.5 mm). Change needle size if necessary to obtain correct gauge. **GAUGE:** 18 sts and 24 rows = 4" (10 cm) in Stockinette stitch (St st)

		FINISHED	CHEST	MEASUREMENT		
	40	**44**	**48**	**52**	**56**	**60"**
4	690	780	865	960	1060	1170 yards MC
4½	765	870	960	1075	1180	1310
5	830	950	1060	1180	1310	1445
5½	900	1040	1155	1305	1435	1620
6	970	1110	1255	1415	1585	1760
4	525	550	590	610	635	665 yards A
4½	535	555	595	620	635	670
5	625	665	690	725	750	785
5½	680	715	760	795	825	855
6	735	765	810	840	885	935

(GAUGE noted along left margin for each group of five rows)

Back and Front
(both alike)

With MC, CO

GAUGE	40	44	48	52	56	60"
4	78	86	94	102	110	118 sts.
4½	90	98	106	114	126	134
5	90	110	118	130	138	150
5½	110	118	130	142	154	162
6	118	130	142	154	166	178

Begin 2x2 Rib; work even until piece measures 2 (2½, 3, 3, 3, 3)" from the beginning, ending with a WS row, increase the following sts evenly spaced across last row:

GAUGE	40	44	48	52	56	60"
4	2	2	2	2	2	2 sts
4½	0	2	2	4	0	2
5	2	0	2	0	2	0
5½	0	4	2	2	0	4
6	2	2	2	2	2	2

Total sts:

GAUGE	40	44	48	52	56	60"
4	80	88	96	104	112	120 sts.
4½	90	100	108	118	126	136
5	100	110	120	130	140	150
5½	110	122	132	144	154	166
6	120	132	144	156	168	180

Next Row (RS): Change to St st; work even until piece measures 15½ (15¾, 16, 16¼, 16½, 16¾)" from the beginning, ending with a WS row.

SHAPE ARMHOLES

Next Row (RS): BO the following sts at beginning of next 2 rows:

GAUGE	40	44	48	52	56	60"
4	3	5	6	8	9	11 sts.
4½	3	5	7	9	10	12
5	4	6	8	10	11	14
5½	4	6	8	11	13	15
6	4	7	9	12	14	16

Decrease Row (RS): K2, k2tog, work to last 4 sts, ssk, k2.

FINISHED CHEST MEASUREMENT	40	44	48	52	56	60"

Repeat Decrease Row every other row

GAUGE	40	44	48	52	56	60"
4	2	3	2	2	2	3 times,
4½	3	3	3	3	3	3
5	3	5	5	5	5	5
5½	3	5	5	6	6	7
6	3	5	6	8	9	9

then every row the following number of times, working WS row decreases as follows: P2, p2tog-tbl, work to last 4 sts, p2tog, p2:

GAUGE	40	44	48	52	56	60"
4	0	1	3	5	7	7 time(s).
4½	0	2	3	5	7	9
5	0	0	2	4	6	8
5½	1	1	3	4	6	8
6	1	2	3	3	4	7

Remaining sts:

GAUGE	40	44	48	52	56	60"
4	68	68	72	72	74	76 sts.
4½	76	78	80	82	84	86
5	84	86	88	90	94	94
5½	92	96	98	100	102	104
6	102	102	106	108	112	114

Work even until armholes measure 6¾ (7¼, 7½, 7¾, 8, 8¼)", ending with a WS row.

SHAPE SHOULDERS

Decrease Row 1 (RS): K2, k2tog, work to last 4 sts, ssk, k2.
Decrease Row 2 (WS): P2, ssp, work to last 4 sts, p2tog, p2.
Decrease 2 sts every row as established

GAUGE	
4	6 times (all sizes).
4½	7
5	8
5½	9
6	10

BO remaining sts on next RS row:

GAUGE	40	44	48	52	56	60"
4	52	52	56	56	58	60 sts.
4½	58	60	62	64	66	68
5	64	66	68	70	74	74
5½	70	74	76	78	80	82
6	78	78	82	84	88	90

Right Sleeve

Using A, CO

GAUGE	40	44	48	52	56	60"
4	38	38	42	42	42	46 sts.
4½	42	42	46	46	46	50
5	46	46	50	50	50	54
5½	50	50	58	58	58	62
6	58	58	62	62	62	66

Begin 2x2 Rib; work even until piece measures 3" from the beginning, ending with a WS row.

FINISHED CHEST MEASUREMENT						
GAUGE	**40**	**44**	**48**	**52**	**56**	**60"**

Next Row (RS): Change to St st, increase the following sts evenly spaced across the first row:

GAUGE	**40**	**44**	**48**	**52**	**56**	**60"**
4	2	2	2	2	2	0 sts.
4½	2	2	2	2	2	2
5	2	2	4	4	4	4
5½	4	4	2	2	2	2
6	0	0	2	2	2	4

Total sts:

GAUGE	40	44	48	52	56	60"
4	40	40	44	44	44	46 sts.
4½	44	44	48	48	48	52
5	48	48	54	54	54	58
5½	54	54	60	60	60	64
6	58	58	64	64	64	70

Work even for 1 row.

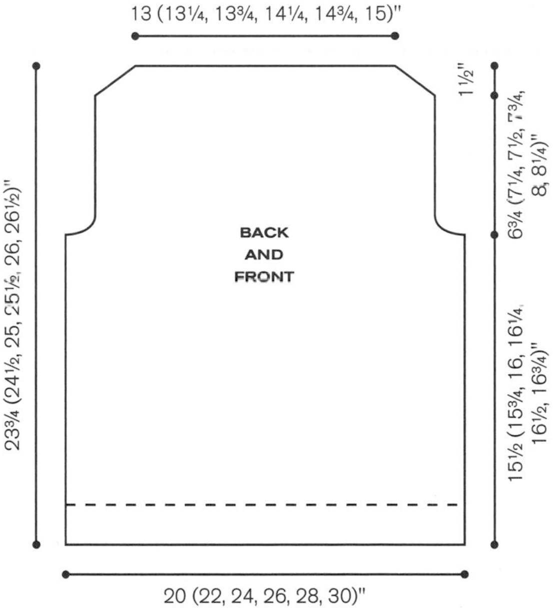

13 (13¼, 13¾, 14¼, 14¾, 15)"

1½"

6¾ (7¼, 7½, 7¾, 8, 8¼)"

15½ (15¾, 16, 16¼, 16½, 16¾)"

23¾ (24½, 25, 25½, 26, 26½)"

BACK AND FRONT

20 (22, 24, 26, 28, 30)"

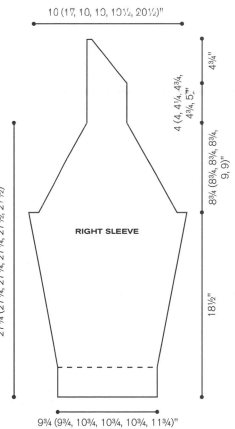

3½"

10 (17, 10, 10, 10½, 20½)"

4¾"

4 (4, 4¼, 4¾, 4¾, 5)"

8¾ (8¾, 8¾, 8¾, 9, 9)"

27¼ (27¼, 27¼, 27¼, 27½, 27½)"

RIGHT SLEEVE

18½"

9¾ (9¾, 10¾, 10¾, 10¾, 11¾)"

BASEBALL JERSEY ■ 85

	40	44	48	52	56	60"

SHAPE SLEEVES

Next Row (RS): Increase 1 st each side this row, and every

GAUGE
4	6	4	4	4	4	4 rows
4½	6	4	4	4	4	4
5	6	4	4	4	4	4
5½	6	4	4	4	4	4
6	6	4	4	4	4	4

GAUGE
4	9	3	3	9	12	15 time(s),
4½	11	3	3	9	15	15
5	14	7	1	10	16	16
5½	14	6	3	12	18	18
6	17	7	4	13	22	22

then every

GAUGE
4	8	6	6	6	6	6 rows
4½	8	6	6	6	6	6
5	8	6	6	6	6	6
5½	8	6	6	6	6	6
6	6	6	6	6	6	6

GAUGE
4	2	10	10	6	4	2 time(s).
4½	2	12	12	8	4	4
5	1	11	15	9	5	5
5½	2	13	15	9	5	5
6	1	14	16	10	4	4

Total sts:

GAUGE
4	64	68	72	76	78	82 sts.
4½	72	76	80	84	88	92
5	80	86	88	94	98	102
5½	88	94	98	104	108	112
6	96	102	106	112	118	124

Work even until piece measures 18½" from the beginning, ending with a WS row.

SHAPE CAP

Next Row (RS): BO the following sts at beginning of next 2 rows:

GAUGE
4	3	5	6	8	9	11 sts.
4½	3	5	7	9	10	12
5	4	6	8	10	11	14
5½	4	6	8	11	13	15
6	4	7	9	12	14	16

Decrease Row (RS): K2, k2tog, work to last 4 sts, ssk, k2.

Repeat Decrease Row every other row

GAUGE
4	21	21	22	22	22	22 times,
4½	24	24	24	24	25	25
5	26	27	26	27	28	27
5½	29	30	30	30	30	30
6	32	32	32	32	33	34

	40	44	48	52	56	60"

Remaining sts:

GAUGE		
4	14 sts (all sizes).
4½	16
5	18
5½	20
6	22

Work even until saddle measures 4 (4, 4¼, 4¾, 4¾, 5)", ending with a RS row.

SHAPE SADDLE

Decrease Row (RS): K1, k2tog, knit to end.

Repeat Decrease Row every row

GAUGE	
4	11 times (all sizes).
4½	13
5	15
5½	17
6	19

BO remaining 2 sts.

Left Sleeve

Work as for Right Sleeve to beginning of Saddle shaping.

SHAPE SADDLE

Decrease Row (RS): Knit to last 3 sts, ssk, k1.

Repeat Decrease Row every other row

GAUGE	
4	12 times (all sizes).
4½	14
5	16
5½	18
6	20

BO remaining 2 sts.

Finishing

Block pieces to measurements. Set in Sleeves. Sew Saddles to Back and Front. Sew side and Sleeve seams.

NECKBAND

Using circ needle and A, pick up and knit the following sts around neck opening:

GAUGE	40	44	48	52	56	60
4	108	108	112	104	108	108 sts.
4½	120	124	124	116	124	120
5	132	140	136	128	140	132
5½	144	156	152	144	148	148
6	164	164	164	156	164	164

Join for working in the rnd, being careful not to twist sts; place marker for beginning of rnd. Begin 2x2 Rib in-the-Rnd; work even for ½ (¾, ¾, ¾, 1, 1)". BO all sts in pattern.

Men Are Babies

FINGERLESS MITTS

Women often suffer for fashion—eyebrow tweezing, bikini waxing, chemical peels, stiletto heels—the list goes on and on. Although this phenomenon is especially relevant for modern-day women, the issue has been around for centuries.

From rib-crushing whalebone corsets to the narrowest hobble skirts, women have willingly bound, squeezed, and pinched themselves throughout history, all in the name of looking good.

Most men, on the other hand, won't put up with discomfort for any reason. Dare we call them babies?

True, Louis XIV and other men of Renaissance Europe wore high heels, rouge, and powdered wigs, but the average modern male won't go for it. Tell your guy that the sweater is snug because that's what they're showing on the runways in Paris and he'll look at you like you're crazy. Show him that style in *Men's Vogue* and he couldn't care less. And it's not just fashion that he will eschew for comfort. Tell him you spun the wool of the sweater you just gave him from the fleece of a lamb his beloved great-grandmother bottle-fed and, if it's the slightest bit itchy, he'll still reject it. For men, comfort trumps fashion and all sentimentality.

So what does this tell you? Well, if you're married to or dating a Renaissance re-enactor or a modern fashionista, you might get him to wear just about anything you make him. But if you're hanging out with a normal, lawn-mowing kind of guy, you should stick to comfortable styles and soft, smooth yarns when knitting for him. No matter how much you like a yarn (or how much you paid for it), your guy is not going to be interested in wearing it—not on his back, his feet, or even his hands—if it doesn't feel good next to his skin. Despite his five-o'clock shadow, calloused palms, and disinterest in romantic comedies, this is one way in which men are sensitive.

Passing the Softness Test

- Before you buy a project's worth of yarn and start knitting, ask your guy to handle a sample ball of it for fifteen minutes (or for as long as he's willing to participate) while he's watching TV. It has to be more than just a quick feel since it can sometimes take a while for sensitivities to show themselves.

- If the yarn passes the hand-holding test, knit up a swatch and have your guy rub it on all the places where the garment will touch his skin to make sure he likes the feel of it.

- Some yarns, such as those made from cashmere goats and llamas, are made from the soft undercoat that grows beneath an outer layer of coarse, exterior guard hairs. It's important to check that these guard hairs were removed properly, as they can be incredibly irritating against the skin if they are spun into the yarn. They're easy to spot in the skein—look for long, firm, protruding hairs.

- Wool made from animals raised for their fleece will be softer than wool from animals raised for meat. You're generally safe if you're buying the yarn at a yarn shop. If you're at a farm or farmer's market and the yarn isn't obviously soft or clearly marked, ask to be sure.

- All yarns made from animal fibers have scales. As a rule of thumb, the more scales on the hair (and the shorter the hairs used to make the yarn), the smoother and finer the yarn will be. From the wool family, merino is typically regarded as the least scratchy since its hairs are short and its scales tiny and numerous.

- A small amount of cashmere in a blend can contribute a bit of softness and add warmth without bulk.

- If, despite your careful selection of yarn, your guy is still complaining that a garment is itchy, try hand-washing it with a little baby shampoo. Rinse well, then soak with a big squirt of ordinary hair conditioner. Repeat, if necessary.

- Synthetic fibers are usually soft without needing any treatment. But if your guy finds them itchy, try machine-washing on a gentle cycle with a little fabric softener added to the rinse.

- As a safety precaution with a hand-knitted sweater, present it with a long-sleeved cotton T-shirt in a matching color. The added layer may quiet any potential complaints about itchiness.

FINGERLESS **MITTS**

These mitts will keep your man's hands warm while leaving his fingers free to operate his camera, grab his tools, or hold onto his bike's handlebars. The ones shown here were knitted in the softest combination of baby alpaca and merino.

Sizes	Small (Medium, Large, X-Large, 2X-Large)
Finished Measurements	8 (8½, 9, 9½, 10)" hand circumference
Notions	Stitch markers; waste yarn
Stitch Pattern	**1x1 Rib** (multiple of 2 sts; 1-rnd repeat) **All Rnds:** *K1, p1; repeat from * to end of rnd.
Notes	This pattern is customizable for multiple sizes and multiple gauges. First make a Stockinette stitch swatch with the yarn you are using to determine appropriate gauge. Then determine the finished hand measurement you want. To make it easier to follow the pattern, you might want to highlight all the numbers that pertain to your chosen gauge and size. Since this pattern is worked in the round, check your gauge in the round (see Special Techniques, page 122). This pattern is written for a set of five double-pointed needles and tells you how to distribute your stitches among them. If you prefer to use circular needles or four double-pointed needles, disregard the stitch distribution instructions.

Yarn Requirements

GAUGE	FINISHED HAND CIRCUMFERENCE				
	8	8½	9	9½	10"
4	100	120	135	155	175 yards
4½	130	155	175	200	225
5	160	190	220	250	280

	FINISHED HAND CIRCUMFERENCE				
	8	8½	9	9½	10"
Cuff — CO					
4	32	34	36	38	40 sts.
4½	36	38	40	42	44
5	40	42	46	48	50

Divide sts evenly among 4 needles:

	8	8½	9	9½	10"
4	8-8-8-8	8-9-8-9	9-9-9-9	9-10-9-10	10-10-10-10
4½	9-9-9-9	9-10-9-10	10-10-10-10	10-11-10-11	11-11-11-11
5	10-10-10-10	10-11-10-11	11-12-11-12	12-12-12-12	12-13-12-13

Join for working in the rnd, being careful not to twist sts; place marker (pm) for beginning of rnd. Begin 1x1 Rib; work even until piece measures 3½ (3¾, 4, 4¼, 4½)" from beginning.

Hand

SHAPE THUMB GUSSET

Rnd 1: K1-f/b, pm, work in pattern from Chart (beginning as indicated below) to last st, pm, k1-f/b:

Begin with rnd number

	8	8½	9	9½	10"
4	15	12	12	9	9,
4½	13	10	10	7	5
5	11	7	7	3	1

st number

	8	8½	9	9½	10"
4	10	9	8	7	6.
4½	8	7	6	5	4
5	6	5	3	2	1

Rnd 2 and all Non-Increase Rnds: Knit to first marker, continue in pattern from Chart to next marker, knit to end.

Increase Rnd: K1-f/b, knit to first marker, work to next marker, knit to last st, k1-f/b.

Repeat Increase Rnd every other rnd

	8	8½	9	9½	10"
4	3	3	3	3	3 times,
4½	4	4	4	4	4
5	5	5	5	5	5

then every 3 rnds 1 (2, 3, 3, 3) time(s).

Total Hand sts:

	8	8½	9	9½	10"
4	44	48	52	54	56 sts.
4½	50	54	58	60	62
5	56	60	66	68	70

FINGERLESS MITTS SHOWN ON FACING PAGE AND PAGE 92.

SIZE: Large; **FINISHED MEASUREMENTS:** 9" circumference; **YARN:** Blue Sky Alpacas Worsted Hand Dyes (50% alpaca / 50% merino; 100 yards / 100 grams): 2 hank(s) #2014 Olive or #2010 Rusty Orange; **NEEDLES:** One set of five double-pointed needles (dpn) size US 8 (5 mm). Change needle size if necessary to obtain correct gauge. **GAUGE:** 16 sts and 25 rnds = 4" (10 cm) in Stockinette stitch (St st)

GAUGE	8	8½	9	9½	10"

Next Rnd: Knit to first marker, work to next marker, k1, transfer the next

GAUGE					
4	12	14	16	16	16 sts
4½	14	16	18	18	18
5	16	18	20	20	20

to waste yarn for Thumb, removing all markers. NOTE: *Half of these transferred sts are from the end of the rnd just completed, and half are from the beginning of the next rnd. You should now have the same number of sts that you CO to begin with.*

Next Rnd: Rejoin for working in the rnd; pm for new beginning of rnd. Work even until Chart is complete. Change to 1x1 Rib; work even for

GAUGE					
4	6	7	9	11	13 rnds.
4½	7	9	11	13	15
5	8	10	12	14	16

BO all sts loosely in pattern.

Thumb

	8	8½	9	9½	10"
Transfer Thumb sts from waste yarn to 3 dpns:					
4	5-5-2	6-5-3	6-6-4	6-6-4	6-6-4
4½	6-5-3	6-6-4	7-7-4	7-7-4	7-7-4
5	6-6-4	7-7-4	8-7-5	8-7-5	8-7-5

GAUGE

Rejoin yarn; begin 1x1 Rib. Work to end. With Needle 3, pick up and knit 2 sts from either side of Thumb gusset.

Total Thumb sts:					
4	14	16	18	18	18 sts.
4½	16	18	20	20	20
5	18	20	22	22	22

GAUGE

Join for working in the rnd; pm for beginning of rnd. Continuing in 1x1 Rib, work even for 6 (7, 9, 11, 12) rnds.
BO all sts loosely in pattern.

KEY

☐ Knit

▣ Purl

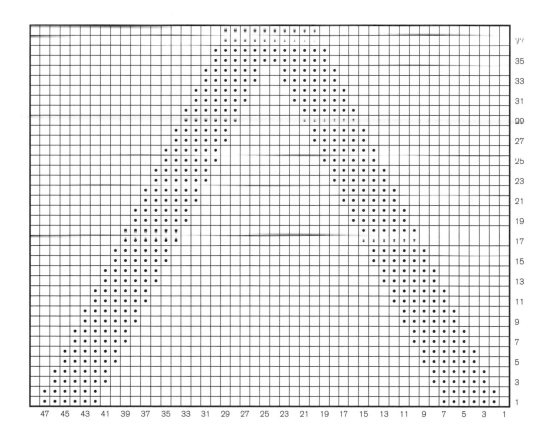

Men Can Compromise

THICK AND WARM SOCKS

Of all the garments a knitter might make for a man, socks are the most immune to his discontent. I've heard from dozens of knitters, and the consensus is that men will wear socks more than any other hand-knitted item. Do all these men have a sock fetish? Or is there some other explanation for this phenomenon?

For most men, it's an easy compromise. They'll wear hand-knitted socks to make the knitters in their lives happy. Why? Because they can keep socks under wraps, inside their boots and shoes, never having to show them off.

Before getting started, there are two issues for a knitter to consider: weight and color. Let's deal with weight first (the yarn's, not your guy's).

While many knitters have an affinity for sock yarn—in fact it has a near-cult following— it just isn't practical for men's socks since it's too light and thin (unless you're making him dress socks, which, trust me, he probably doesn't want). Men like hand-knitted socks that are thick, warm, and comfortable—socks they can wear padding around the house, hiking, walking the dog, golfing, etc. Even yarn manufacturers admit, though probably without realizing it, that sock yarn isn't meant for men's socks. On most labels it says that one ball of sock yarn makes one pair of socks. Not in a men's size 11 it doesn't, and there are a lot of 12s and 13s walking around out there, too.

Color is also a challenge when choosing yarn for men's socks. For this I turned to the members of my group, Unwinding Men, on Ravelry.com.

"I guess for socks, most anything goes color-wise," wrote Heidi from Chicago. "He has started to pick out some brighter colors for socks than he chooses for sweaters."

"DBF is a fan of blues, grays, and whites," reported Kristin from Maryland. So she was surprised that he liked her choice of bright red cuffs, heels, and toes. (I reminded her that the red parts are hidden when he's wearing shoes and pants.)

"He likes much more vibrant-colored socks than the rest of his clothes," Michele in San Diego wrote about her fiancé. "I was working on some very bright blue and purple ones with a crazy slip stitch argyle pattern (originally intended for his mom) that he ended up claiming as his own."

Clearly the acceptance of brighter colors was a surprise to these women. It was a huge relief to Lynne in Washington who claimed, "I CANNOT work with drab colors."

My favorite story came from Sally in Wales who let her husband help dye the yarn for his socks. "He fell in love with all the pretty colors," she said. "Now the socks look like a rainbow exploded all over his feet."

One word of caution. While these stories can be encouraging, don't surprise your guy with socks that are outside of his typical color range. Before you start, show him the colors online or take him to the store (if he's willing to go), so he can choose for himself. Even then, show him a knitted swatch just to be sure. Better safe than sorry.

Knitting Men's Socks

- Don't pick itchy yarn, or yarn with a halo, such as mohair. Think simple, soft, and not too thin (or too thick).

- Pick a machine-washable yarn. He's more likely to wear the socks if they're clean. And he's more likely to wash them if he can throw them in the machine.

- If you're making cotton-blend socks, make them 1" smaller than his actual foot diameter. Cotton has no memory and even in a blend it won't bounce back very well when stretched. Plus cotton and cotton-blend socks just feel better when they're a little snug.

- Men's socks need to be knitted tightly in order to be useful. To achieve, experiment with needles one size smaller than the yarn label suggests, and go down from there. You shouldn't be able to see through the stitches, even when the fabric is stretched.

- If the socks are a gift or you simply can't get your man to try them on, check the sizing chart on page 102.

- Unless you naturally cast on very loosely, cast on for socks holding two needles together instead of just one needle. This will give you a looser cast-on row that will not pull in, pinch, or roll down your man's calf.

- For extra strength in the heels and toes, hold a strand of polyester thread in a coordinating color with your yarn as you work these sections. Begin using the thread when you start the heel flap, and continue until you have worked the gussets. Add the thread again when you begin to shape the toes.

- If you can, have him try on the socks after knitting the calf, then after turning the heel, and again before shaping the toes. If he balks, slip them on his feet while he's sleeping.

- If your man complains about feeling the purl bumps on the sole of his foot when he walks (some men have very sensitive feet), simply purl every stitch on Needles 1 and 2 (the sole of his foot) after knitting the gussets. This will put the knit (or flat side) of the stockinette against the sole of his foot.

- When knitting right- and left-fitting socks, add a contrasting color thread to reinforce the toe of one sock. It will show on the outside of the sock, and your guy will always know which sock goes on which foot. It may seem obvious to you, but men are oblivious (see Rule #9, page 108).

- Consider the following uses for socks worked at different gauges:

Gauge	Use
3 sts per inch	House socks
3½ sts per inch	Hiking or work boot socks
4 sts per inch	Sneaker or tennis shoe socks
4½ sts per inch	Golf shoe socks
5 sts per inch	Casual or weekend shoe socks
5½ sts per inch	Cowboy boot socks

THICK AND WARM **SOCKS**

These socks start with a rib to keep them up. The rest of the leg and foot follow a simple stockinette-stitch pattern. Also included (as a variation at the end of the pattern) are instructions for shaping the socks for the right and left foot. I like this refinement a lot—it gives me a small challenge when I'm knitting and socks shaped this way are more comfortable, less likely to wear out at the toe, and hold their form longer than unshaped socks. But if you think the extra thought required when putting on the socks will turn your guy off, skip it.

Sizes	**Man's Shoe Size**	9	10	11	12	13	14+	
	Foot Circumference	9	9½	9½	10	10½	11"	
	For wide feet or a high instep, go up 1 or 2 sizes.							
	Man's Height	5'8" and under	5'9"	5'10"	5'11"	6'	6'1"	6'2" and taller
	Sock Leg Length	7½	8	8½	9	9½	10	10½"
	NOTE: Leg length is measured from CO edge to beginning of Heel Flap.							

Notions	Stitch marker (optional)
Abbreviations	**Srk2tog-tbl:** Slip next st knitwise to right-hand needle, return st to left-hand needle in its new orientation, knit 2 sts together through back loops.
Stitch Pattern	**1x1 Rib** (multiple of 2 sts; 1-row/rnd repeat) **All Rows/Rnds:** *K1, p1; repeat from * to end.

SOCKS SHOWN ABOVE AND PAGE 107.
SIZE: 10 shoe; **FINISHED MEASUREMENTS:** 9½" Foot circumference, 10½" Foot length from back of Heel, 9" Leg length to beginning of Heel Flap; **YARN:** ShiBuiKnits Merino Worsted (100% superwash merino; 191 yards / 100 grams): 2 hanks #MW06 Ink or #MW7498 Seaweed; **NEEDLES:** One pair straight needles size US 6 (4 mm), one set of five double-pointed needles (dpn) size US 6 (4 mm). Change needle size if necessary to obtain correct gauge. **GAUGE:** 20 sts and 26 rnds = 4" (10 cm) in Stockinette stitch (St st)

Notes

This pattern is customizable for multiple sizes and multiple gauges. First make a Stockinette stitch swatch with the yarn you are using to determine appropriate gauge (see the chart on page 101 for best gauges to use for different sock types). Since this pattern is worked in the round, check your gauge in the round (see Special Techniques, page122). Then determine the desired foot circumference or shoe size and leg length from the tables on facing page. To make it easier to follow the pattern, you might want to highlight all the numbers that pertain to your chosen gauge and size.

Yarn Requirements

NOTE: Yarn requirements are based on a leg length of 9", and a foot length of 10½" from back of heel. If you plan on working a shorter leg and/or foot length, you may not require as much yarn as shown. If you plan on working a longer leg and/or foot length, you should purchase additional yarn.

GAUGE	FINISHED FOOT CIRCUMFERENCE				
	9	9½	10	10½	11"
3	440	515	515	605	605 yards
3½	570	570	645	645	730
4	615	615	690	690	770
4½	675	675	740	800	820
5	580	635	635	705	760
5½	770	845	915	915	990

Leg

Using 2 straight needles held together, CO

GAUGE					
3	24	28	28	32	32 sts.
3½	32	32	36	36	40
4	36	36	40	40	44
4½	40	40	44	48	48
5	44	48	48	52	56
5 ½	48	52	56	56	60

Slip 1 needle from CO row. Begin 1x1 Rib; working back and forth, work even for 3 rows. Divide sts evenly among 4 dpns. Join for working in the rnd, being careful not to twist sts; place marker (pm) for beginning of rnd (optional). NOTE: *The beginning of the rnd will always be at the gap between two needles, where the tail hangs from the bottom of the knitting; this can serve as a marker, if preferred.* Continuing in 1x1 Rib, work even in rnds until piece measures 3" from the beginning.

Next Rnd: Change to St st (knit every rnd); work even to desired leg length (see chart on opposite page).

Heel Flap

Set-Up Row 1 (RS): Knit

GAUGE					
3	6	7	7	8	8 sts, turn work.
3½	8	8	9	9	10
4	9	9	10	10	11
4½	10	10	11	12	12
5	11	12	12	13	14
5½	12	13	14	14	15

Set-Up Row 2: Slip 1, purl across Needles 1 and 4. Leave remaining sts on Needles 2 and 3 for instep.
Row 1 (RS): Working only on Heel Flap sts, *slip 1, k1; repeat from * to end.
Row 2: Slip 1, purl to end.
Repeat Rows 1 and 2 until you have worked as many rows in your Heel Flap as you have Heel Flap sts, ending with a WS row.

Turn Heel

Set-Up Row 1: Knit all sts from Needle 4, k2 from Needle 1 (k1 if there are fewer than 16 sts on Heel Flap needles), ssk, k1, turn.
Set-Up Row 2: P6 (p4 if there are fewer than 16 sts on Heel Flap needles), p2tog, p1, turn.
Row 1: Knit to 1 st before gap, ssk [the 2 sts on either side of gap], k1, turn.
Row 2: Purl to 1 st before gap, p2tog [the 2 sts on either side of gap], p1, turn.
Repeat Rows 1 and 2 until all Heel Flap sts have been worked. NOTE: *For some sizes, you will not have enough sts to work the final k1 and p1 sts in the last repeat of Rows 1 and 2; simply omit them.*

FINISHED FOOT CIRCUMFERENCE

GAUGE	9	9½	10	10½	11"
Remaining sts:					
3	8	8	8	10	10 sts
3½	10	10	12	12	12
4	12	12	12	12	14
4½	12	12	14	14	14
5	14	14	14	16	16
5½	16	16	18	18	18

Gusset

Next Row (RS): Needle 1: Knit across needle, pick up and knit 1 st along left side of Heel Flap for every 2 rows worked in the Heel Flap, M1; **Needles 2 and 3:** Knit across sts on instep needles; **Needle 4:** M1, pick up and knit sts along right side of Heel Flap as for left side, knit to end of needle; pm for beginning of rnd.

GAUGE	Total sts:				
3	34	38	38	44	44 sts.
3½	44	44	50	50	54
4	50	50	54	54	60
4½	54	54	60	64	64
5	60	64	64	70	74
5½	64	70	74	74	80

Next Rnd: Needle 1: Knit to last 2 sts, k2tog; **Needles 2 and 3:** Knit; **Needle 4:** Ssk, knit to end.
Decrease Rnd: Needle 1: Knit to last 3 sts, k2tog, k1; **Needles 2 and 3:** Knit; **Needle 4:** K1, ssk, knit to end. Work even for 1 rnd.
Repeat Decrease Rnd every other rnd until there are the same number of sts on each needle, and the total number of sts is the number you CO.

Foot

Work even until piece measures 2" less than desired length from back of Heel, or to length given below:

Shoe Size	9	9½	10	10½	11	11½	12	13	14
Length	7½	7¾	8	8 ¼	8½	8¾	9	9½	10"

Toe	**Decrease Rnd: Needle 1:** Knit to last 3 sts, ssk, k1; **Needle 2:** K1, k2tog, knit to end; **Needle 3:** Knit to last 3 sts, ssk, k1; **Needle 4:** K1, k2tog, knit to end. Knit 1 rnd. Repeat Decrease Rnd every other rnd until you have half the number of sts you started with. Repeat Decrease Rnd every rnd until ½" of sts remain on each needle. Knit to end of Needle 1.
Finishing	Break yarn, leaving long tail. Transfer sts from Needle 1 to Needle 4, and sts from Needle 3 to Needle 2. Using Kitchener st (see Special Techniques, page 122), graft Toe sts. Using tail from CO, close gap at CO edge. Block lightly.
VARIATION	**MAKING RIGHT AND LEFT SOCKS**
Right Sock	Work as above to ¼" before beginning of Toe shaping. **Decrease Rnd 1: Needle 1:** Knit to last 3 sts, k2tog, k1; **Needle 2:** K1, srk2tog-tbl, knit to end; **Needles 3 and 4:** Knit to end. Knit 1 rnd. Repeat Decrease Rnd 1 every other rnd until you have roughly ¼ fewer sts than you started with. NOTE: *As you repeat this Decrease Rnd, you may find that you do not have enough sts left on Needles 1 and 2 to complete the Decrease Rnd; simply work the last st on Needle 4 together with the first st on Needle 1, and the last st on Needle 2 together with the first st on Needle 3.* **Decrease Rnd 2.** Slide enough sts from Needle 4 to Needle 1 and from Needle 3 to Needle 2 so that you now have the same number of sts on all needles; you may have 1 extra st each on Needles 3 and 4. NOTE: *You may find you need to do this again as you work additional Decrease Rnds.* **Needle 1:** Knit to last 3 sts, k2tog, k1; **Needle 2:** K1, srk2tog-tbl, knit to end; **Needle 3:** Knit to last 3 sts, k2tog, k1; **Needle 4:** K1, srk2tog-tbl, knit to end. Knit 1 rnd. Repeat Decrease Rnd 2 every other rnd once, Decrease Rnd 1 every other rnd once, then Decrease Rnd 2 every rnd until 8 or 10 sts remain. Knit to end of Needle 1.
Left Sock	Work as above to ¼" before beginning of Toe shaping, ending with Needle 2. Renumber needles so that next needle is now Needle 1, then 2, 3, and 4. Complete as for Right Sock.
Finishing	Break yarn, leaving long tail. Transfer sts from Needle 1 to Needle 4, and sts from Needle 3 to Needle 2. Using Kitchener st, graft Toe sts. Weave in ends. Block lightly.

Men **Are** Oblivious

REVERSIBLE **CABLE SCARF**

Take this quiz:

You're out to lunch with a girlfriend and she arrives with her blouse misbuttoned (accidentally of course). Do you . . .

A: Say nothing?

B: Reach out and rebutton her blouse right there at the hostess stand?

C: Tell her later that night on the phone?

D: Find a way to discreetly let her know so she can fix the problem herself?

The only civilized and acceptable answer, of course, is D.

Now try again:

You're going out for the evening with your man and his tie is askew. He's never been able to tie it right, and as always the knot is lopsided and the tie is hanging off to the side. He says he's ready to go. Do you . . .

A: Say nothing, pretend it's perfect, and enjoy your evening?

B: Step forward and take his tie off, remaking it yourself?

C: Not say a word, but straighten it for him in public later when you can't bear looking at it any longer?

D: Tell him to keep trying until he gets it right?

The only way to guarantee you'll have a fun night is to choose answer A.

There is nothing more annoying to a man than being told he doesn't look right. Actually, there is something more annoying: being fussed over in public, which most men find humiliating.

Men and Scarves

- No man wants to look like Isadora Duncan—his scarf blowing in the wind behind him. So don't knit him scarves longer than he is tall, unless he's interested in learning how to wrap it correctly (see next note).

- To properly wrap a long scarf, double the scarf by putting both ends together. Put the scarf around the neck and pull the two ends together through the loop on the other side. Pull to tighten up to collarbone. This look works with jeans, sport coats, and overcoats.

- Older or more conservative men tend to prefer shorter scarves, sometimes called mufflers. Mufflers don't stick out from the bottom of their jackets, so if your conservative guy wears a coat, knit him a muffler that comes just to his waist.

- Beware of scarves that are too wide. Anything over 10" wide falls into the shawl category and should be avoided at all costs. Plus the wider you make his scarf the warmer it's going to keep him, and most men just don't need that much insulation.

- Men's necks are particularly sensitive, so only use very soft yarn for scarves.

- Men don't shave all the time, so don't pick a yarn that will pill or pull easily on his beard, like mohair or loosely spun cotton. This will leave bits of fuzz stuck to his neck and face when he removes the scarf.

Except for a brief period in 18th-century Europe when men wore rouge and powdered wigs, guys have typically never fussed much over their appearance. So, if you make a man a cabled scarf, be prepared to see it hanging with the "wrong" side facing front, and if you make him a sweater, know that he may wear it backwards sometimes.

It's not that men don't care. It's just that they don't always pay attention. I was reminded of this one afternoon when, after racing around doing chores and running errands, I met some friends for lunch. I was sitting in the restaurant enjoying a beer when I realized my polo shirt was on inside out. It didn't bother me too much, but I had to wonder. Did Mark not notice when we got in the car? And what about the postmaster or the guy who cashed my check at the bank? Sure, maybe. But truth be told, men just don't tend to focus on this kind of stuff, and even if they do notice, they don't usually mention it because it doesn't seem important.

Now picture your man sitting with his friends, shirt inside out, sweater on backwards, or committing any other clothing faux pas you can imagine. It bothers you, doesn't it? Well, when it comes to knitwear, there are ways to prevent some of these classic clothing mishaps. A simple label sewn into the inside back neck of a handknit sweater can be a tremendous help. Knitting one row at the cuff of a hand warmer in a contrasting color can let him know which is the right or left one (if it's close to the cuff, it will be hidden up his sleeve when he's wearing it). The same thing can work at the toe on a sock if you knit him right- and left-fitting socks (see page 106). Or you can knit him a cabled scarf that's completely reversible, so no matter how much he rushes or how little attention he pays, he'll always have his best side facing forward.

REVERSIBLE **CABLE SCARF**

The narrow, reversible cables in this scarf make it thick, warm, and masculine. It's shown here at two different lengths (56" and 90"). You can, of course, make it any length your man likes as long as you adjust the yarn quantity accordingly. At right are guidelines for varying the gauge so you can use this pattern with many types of yarn.

Finished Measurements	7" wide x 56 (90)" long
Yarn	Claudia Hand Painted Yarns Sport (100% merino; 225 yards / 100 grams): 3 (4) hanks Navy Olive (Honey)
Needles	One pair straight needles size US 5 (3.75 mm) Change needle size if necessary to obtain correct gauge.
Notions	Cable needle (cn)
Gauge	24 sts and 26 rows = 4" (10 cm) in 1x1 Rib
Abbreviations	**C8F-p:** Slip 4 sts to cn, hold to front, [p1, k1] twice, [p1, k1] twice from cn. **C12F-p:** Slip 6 sts to cn, hold to front, [p1, k1] 3 times, [p1, k1] 3 times from cn. **C12F-k:** Slip 6 sts to cn, hold to front, [k1, p1] 3 times, [k1, p1] 3 times from cn. **C12B-p:** Slip 6 sts to cn, hold to back, [p1, k1] 3 times, [p1, k1] 3 times from cn. **C12B-k:** Slip 6 sts to cn, hold to back, [k1, p1] 3 times, [k1, p1] 3 times from cn.
Cable Pattern	(panel of 74 sts; 8-row repeat) **Row 1 (RS):** K1, p1, k1, C12F-p, [p1, k1] 9 times, C8F-p, p1, *k1, p1; repeat from * to end. **Rows 2, 4, and 6:** *K1, p1; repeat from * to end. **Row 3:** [K1, p1] 22 times, C12F-k, *k1, p1; repeat from * to end. **Row 5:** [K1, p1] 9 times, C12B-k, k1, p1, k1, C8F-p, p1, *k1, p1; repeat from * to end. **Row 7:** K1, [p1, k1] 29 times, C12B-p, p1, k1, p1. **Row 8:** Repeat Row 2. Repeat Rows 1-8 for Cable Pattern.

CHANGING **THE GAUGE**

This scarf is 7" wide at the suggested gauge of 6 stitches per inch over a 1x1 Rib. Here are some guidelines to follow if you want to work with a yarn at a different gauge. Remember, if you decide to change the length or width of the scarf, you may need to purchase additional yarn to complete the project.

- If your gauge is 6½ or (heaven help you) 7 stitches per inch over a 1x1 Rib, your scarf will be only 5" to 6" wide. This is fine for the longer version or a smaller guy. But for the shorter scarf, consider putting another small cable down the center to increase the width. To do this, simply cast on 10 more stitches than called for in the pattern, for a total of 84 stitches. Working only from the chart, work 43 stitches (including cables already indicated in the Chart), repeat stitches 34 through 43, then continue to the end.

- If your gauge is a chunky 4 to 5 stitches per inch over the 1x1 Rib, your scarf will be as wide as 8" to 10". This is fine for the shorter version, but consider removing the center cable at this gauge in the longer version. To do this, simply cast on 10 fewer stitches than called for in the pattern, for a total of 64 stitches. Then omit stitches 34 through 43 from the Chart.

Scarf | CO 74 sts. Begin Cable Pattern (you may follow the text or Chart); work even until 45 (73) vertical repeats of pattern have been complete, or until scarf measures 56 (90)". BO all sts in pattern.

Finishing | Weave in ends.
Do not block.

KEY

☐ Knit on RS, purl on WS.

⊡ Purl on RS, knit on WS.

C8F-p: Slip 4 sts to cn, hold to front, [p1, k1] twice, [p1, k1] twice from cn.

C12F-p: Slip 6 sts to cn, hold to front, [p1, k1] 3 times, [p1, k1] 3 times from cn.

C12F-k: Slip 6 sts to cn, hold to front, [k1, p1] 3 times, [k1, p1] 3 times from cn.

C12B-p: Slip 6 sts to cn, hold to back, [p1, k1] 3 times, [p1, k1] 3 times from cn.

C12B-k: Slip 6 sts to cn, hold to back, [k1, p1] 3 times, [k1, p1] 3 times from cn.

CABLE PATTERN CHART

When In **Doubt, Make** Him Something **Basic**

WATCH CAP

There are all sorts of men walking the planet, from wild young college students to conservative bankers to fashion-backward dads. But when it comes to clothes, there is one trait they all have in common: They will never complain if you make them something basic. Season after season, year after year, stores like Eddie Bauer, Lands' End, and Banana Republic continue to offer basic knit sweaters, scarves, and hats because men, regardless of age, background, or financial status, continue to buy and wear them. As knitters, we must learn from this.

Think of it this way: Men get used to wearing a suit and tie to work and/or for special occasions and then figure out that it's easy to stick to a uniform of some sort all the time. On top of that, men almost always get more conservative with age.

Richard, the co-owner (with his wife Barbara) of my local yarn shop, proves my point. The first time I walked into their store, I couldn't help but notice that Barbara looked very hip, layered all in black with short, spiky silver hair, while Richard appeared conservative in a simple navy cardigan, which, oddly enough, seemed to be machine-made.

After I befriended the two, I quickly learned that Richard had once been a bona fide hippie and had colorful tales to tell about Woodstock, free love, and transcendental meditation. A true product of the 1960s, Richard was even assigned the title "Governor of the Age of Enlightenment" by the famed Beatles' guru, Maharishi Mahesh Yogi. But, over the years, Richard gave up his love beads and traded in his Birkenstocks for khakis and simple dark sweaters. And now, in his sixties, Richard likes his navy blue Banana Republic sweater more than anything.

I once asked Barbara if she had ever knitted Richard a sweater and she informed me that he likes a tight gauge.

"And I am not knitting him a sweater at 7 stitches to the inch," she added with finality.

However, I did notice that Richard always had a knitted cap either on his head or tucked into his back pocket.

"Did you make *that*?" I asked her.

"I did," she said. "It's the only handknit thing he'll wear."

I borrowed the hat from Richard to have a better look, and indeed, it was beautiful, warm, and so tightly knit that it could have passed as machine-made. I knew instantly that it would appeal to all men—businessmen, snowboarders, and grandfathers alike. After all, that is another trait all men have in common; their heads *will* get cold in winter. I spent weeks examining Richard's hat and playing with the design, adding a long brim that folds and trying different yarns. But I always kept the gauge tight and the details simple. The result is the Watch Cap presented here. It could, quite feasibly, please every man on the planet.

WATCH **CAP**

This classic hat will never go out of style and can be made with or without the fold-up brim. The hat shown is made with a soft, warm yak-merino blend.

Sizes	Small (Medium, Large)
Finished Measurements	18 (21, 24)" circumference
Notions	Stitch marker
Stitch Pattern	**1x1 Rib** (multiple of 2 sts; 1-rnd repeat) **All Rnds:** *K1, p1; repeat from * to end of rnd.
Notes	This pattern is customizable for multiple sizes and multiple gauges, in addition to Short Rib and Long Rib. First make a Stockinette stitch swatch with the yarn you are using to determine appropriate gauge. Then determine the circumference you want and whether you want Short Rib or Long Rib. To make it easier to follow the pattern, you might want to highlight all the numbers that pertain to your chosen gauge and size.

Yarn Requirements

		FINISHED CIRCUMFERENCE		
		18	**21**	**24"**
SHORT RIB	3	80	105	135 yards
G A U G E	4	95	125	160
	5	115	150	190
	6	130	180	230
	7	155	200	260
LONG RIB	3	115	135	170 yards
G A U G E	4	160	165	270
	5	200	260	325
	6	225	310	385
	7	270	340	440

Hat

GAUGE

Using circ needle, CO

	18	21	24"
3	54	64	72 sts.
4	72	84	96
5	92	104	118
6	108	130	144
7	130	148	170

Join for working in the rnd, being careful not to twist sts; place marker (pm) for beginning of rnd. Begin 1x1 Rib; work even until piece measures 3 (3½, 4)" from the beginning [6 (6½, 7)" for the Long Rib].

Decrease the following sts evenly across rnd:

GAUGE

3	0	1	0 st(s).
4	0	0	0
5	1	0	1
6	4	0	1
7	0	5	1

Remaining sts:

GAUGE

3	54	60	72 sts.
4	72	84	96
5	91	104	117
6	104	130	143
7	130	143	169

Next Rnd: Change to St st; work even until piece measures 5 (6, 7)" from the beginning [8 (9, 10)" for the Long Rib].

SHAPE CROWN

Rnd 1: *Knit

GAUGE

3	7 sts (all sizes), k2tog; repeat from * to end.
4	10
5	11
6	11
7	11

Remaining sts:

GAUGE

3	48	56	64 sts.
4	66	77	88
5	84	96	108
6	96	120	132
7	120	132	156

Rnd 2 and all even-numbered Rnds: Knit.

WATCH CAP SHOWN ON FACING PAGE AND ON PAGE 120.

SIZE: Medium; FINISHED MEASUREMENTS: 21" circumference; YARN: Karabella Superyak (50% extrafine merino / 50% yak; 125 yards / 50 grams): Short Rib: 1 hank #10153; Long Rib: 1 (2, 2) hank(s) #10204; NEEDLES: One 12" (30 cm) long circular (circ) needle size US 8 (5 mm), one set of four double-pointed needles (dpn) size US 8 (5 mm). Change needle size if necessary to obtain correct gauge. GAUGE: 16 sts and 25 rows = 4" (10 cm) in Stockinette stitch (St st)

	18	21	24"

Rnd 3: *Knit

GAUGE

	18	21	24"
3	6 sts (all sizes), k2tog; repeat from * to end.		
4	9		
5	10		
6	10		
7	10		

Remaining sts:

GAUGE

	18	21	24"
3	42	49	56 sts.
4	60	70	80
5	77	88	99
6	88	110	121
7	110	121	143

Continue working decreases in this manner, knitting 1 less st between decreases, until the following sts remain:

GAUGE

	18	21	24"
3	12	14	16 sts.
4	12	14	16
5	14	16	18
6	16	20	22
7	20	22	26

Next Rnd: *K2tog; repeat from * to end. Remaining sts:

GAUGE

	18	21	24"
3	6	7	8 sts.
4	6	7	8
5	7	8	9
6	8	10	11
7	10	11	13

Break yarn, leaving a long tail. Thread tail through remaining sts, pull tight and fasten off, with tail to WS.

Special Techniques

Cable CO: Make a loop (using a slip knot) with the working yarn and place it on the left-hand needle (first st CO), knit into slip knot, draw up a loop but do not drop st from left-hand needle; place new loop on left-hand needle; *insert the tip of the right-hand needle into the space between the last 2 sts on the left-hand needle and draw up a loop; place the loop on the left-hand needle. Repeat from * for remaining sts to be CO, or for casting on at the end of a row in progress.

Garter Stitch: Knit every row when working straight; knit 1 round, purl 1 round when working circular.

Getting Your Gauge in the Round: We often knit our swatches flat, even if the garment we are making is worked in the round. The problem with this system is that it is possible to knit at a different gauge when working back and forth than when knitting in the round. For instance, if working Stockinette st flat, you will knit one row, purl one row, but will knit all rounds if working in the round. If your knits are looser than your purls, for instance, your two gauges will be different. Follow the instructions below to swatch in the round if you will be working in the round. For a garment that requires both flat knitting and knitting in the round, it is a good idea to test your gauge both ways to ensure accuracy.

To check your gauge in the round, using a double-pointed needle, cast on 6" worth of stitches. Knit your first row. Do not turn. Slide your knitting to the other end of the needle. Bring the working yarn across the back from the left end of the needle to the right and use it to knit across the row once again, making sure you don't pull the yarn too tightly or your work will pucker. You will have a loose float of yarn on the back; that's okay. Repeat this until you have knit 6". Remove the needles and measure your gauge over the center 4".

Joining in the Round: To avoid creating a Mobius when you join your knitting in the round, work the first two rows back and forth as you would if you weren't working the piece in the round. The first row will be a RS row and the second will be a WS row. Join your

knitting to work in the round after you have worked the second row. Later, when you are done with the garment, use the CO tail to sew up the tiny 2-row opening.

Kitchener Stitch: Using a blunt tapestry needle, thread a length of yarn approximately 4 times the length of the section to be joined. Hold the pieces to be joined wrong sides together, with the needles holding the sts parallel, both ends pointing to the right. Working from right to left, insert tapestry needle into first st on front needle as if to purl, pull yarn through, leaving st on needle; insert tapestry needle into first st on back needle as if to knit, pull yarn through, leaving st on needle; *insert tapestry needle into first st on front needle as if to knit, pull yarn through, remove st from needle; insert tapestry needle into next st on front needle as if to purl, pull yarn through, leave st on needle; insert tapestry needle into first st on back needle as if to purl, pull yarn through, remove st from needle; insert tapestry needle into next st on back needle as if to knit, pull yarn through, leave st on needle. Repeat from *, working 3 or 4 sts at a time, then go back and adjust tension to match the pieces being joined. When 1 st remains on each needle, cut yarn and pass through last 2 sts to fasten off.

Knitting in the Round on Two Circular Needles: If you find double-pointed needles tricky to use (or easy to drop and lose), try knitting in the round on 2 circular needles. You'll start the first inch of ribbing with double-pointed needles since they are easier to maneuver in the first few rows, then switch to circular needles.

Round 1: Using a 12" or 16" circular needle of the same size as your double-pointed needles, work the stitches off the first 2 double-pointed needles. Using a second circular needle of the same length and size as the first, work the stitches off the remaining 2 double-pointed needles.

Turn both needles together so the working yarn is in the back on the right-hand side. Pull the yarn forward and work across the front needle, using both ends of the front needle and leaving the back needle just sitting there waiting for you. You will never knit from one circular needle to the other. Turn the knitting and repeat the process, using what is now the front needle. It will take 2 passes of the "front" needle to do an entire round.

Reading Charts: Unless otherwise specified in the instructions, when working straight, charts are read from right to left for RS rows, from left to right for WS rows. Row numbers are written at the beginning of each row. Numbers on the right indicate RS rows; numbers on the left indicate WS rows. When working circular, all rounds are read from right to left.

Reverse Stockinette Stitch (Rev St st): Purl on RS rows, knit on WS rows when working straight, purl every round when working circular.

Ribbing: Although rib stitch patterns use different numbers of stitches, all are worked in the same way. The instructions will specify how many stitches to knit or purl; the example below uses k1, p1
Row/Rnd 1: *K1, p1; repeat from * across, (end k1 if an odd number of sts).
Row/Rnd 2: Knit the knit sts and purl the purl sts as they face you.
Repeat Row/Rnd 2 for rib stitch.

Stockinette Stitch (St st): Knit on RS rows, purl on WS rows when working straight; knit every round when working circular.

Three-Needle BO: Place the sts to be joined onto two same-size needles; hold the pieces to be joined with the right sides facing each other and the needles parallel, both pointing to the right. Holding both needles in your left hand, using working yarn and a third needle same size or one size larger, insert third needle into first st on front needle, then into first st on back needle; knit these 2 sts together; *knit next st from each needle together (2 sts on right-hand needle); pass first st over second st to BO 1 st. Repeat from * until 1 st remains on third needle; cut yarn and fasten off.

Abbreviations

BO – Bind off

Circ – Circular

Cn – Cable needle

CO – Cast on

Dpn(s) – Double-pointed needle(s)

K – Knit

K1b – Knit into stitch below next stitch on needle.

K1-f/b – Knit into front loop and back loop of same stitch to increase 1 stitch.

K2tog – Knit 2 stitches together.

M1 – With tip of left-hand needle inserted from front to back, lift strand between 2 needles onto left-hand needle; knit strand through back loop to increase 1 stitch.

P2tog – Purl 2 stitches together.

Pm – Place marker

P – Purl

Rnd(s) – Round(s)

RS – Right side

S2kp2 – Slip next 2 stitches together to right-hand needle as if to knit 2 together, k1, pass 2 slipped stitches over.

Sm – Slip marker

Ssk (slip, slip, knit) – Slip next 2 stitches to right-hand needle 1 at a time as if to knit; return them to left-hand needle 1 at a time in their new orientation; knit them together through the back loops.

Ssp (slip, slip, purl) – Slip next 2 sts to right-hand needle one at a time as if to knit; return them to left-hand needle one at a time in their new orientation; purl them together through the back loops.

St(s) – Stitch(es)

Tog – Together

WS – Wrong side

Wyib – With yarn in back

Wyif – With yarn in front

Yarn Sources

Berroco, Inc.
14 Elmdale Road
PO Box 367
Uxbridge, MA 01569
800-343-4948
www.berroco.com

Blue Sky Alpacas, Inc.
PO Box 88
Cedar, MN 55011
888-460-8862
www.blueskyalpacas.com

Classic Elite Yarns, Inc.
122 Western Avenue
Lowell, MA 01851
800-343-0308
www.classiceliteyarns.com

Claudia Hand Painted Yarns
40 West Washington Street
Harrisonburg, VA 22802
540-433-1140
www.claudiaco.com

GGH
(Distributed by Muench Yarns)
1323 Scott Street
Petaluma, CA 94954
800-733-9276
www.muenchyarns.com

Jo Sharp
(Distributed by Knitting Fever)
35 Debevoise Avenue
Roosevelt, NY 11575
800-645-3457
www.knittingfever.com

Karabella Yarns, Inc.
1201 Broadway
New York, NY 10001
800-550-0898
www.karabellayarns.com

Misti Alpaca
Misti International, Inc.
PO Box 2532
Glen Ellyn, IL 60138
888-776-9276
www.mistialpaca.com

O-Wool
The Vermont Organic Fiber Company
52 Seymour Street
Middlebury, VT 05753
802-388-1313
www.o-wool.com

Plymouth Yarn Company
500 Lafayette Street
Bristol, PA 19007
215-788-0459
www.plymouthyarn.com

Rowan Yarns
(Distributed by Westminster Fibers)
165 Ledge Street
Nashua, NH 03060
800-445-9276
www.knitrowan.com

ShiBui
ShibuiKnits, LLC
1101 SW Alder Street
Portland, OR 97205
503-595-5898
www.shibuiknits.com

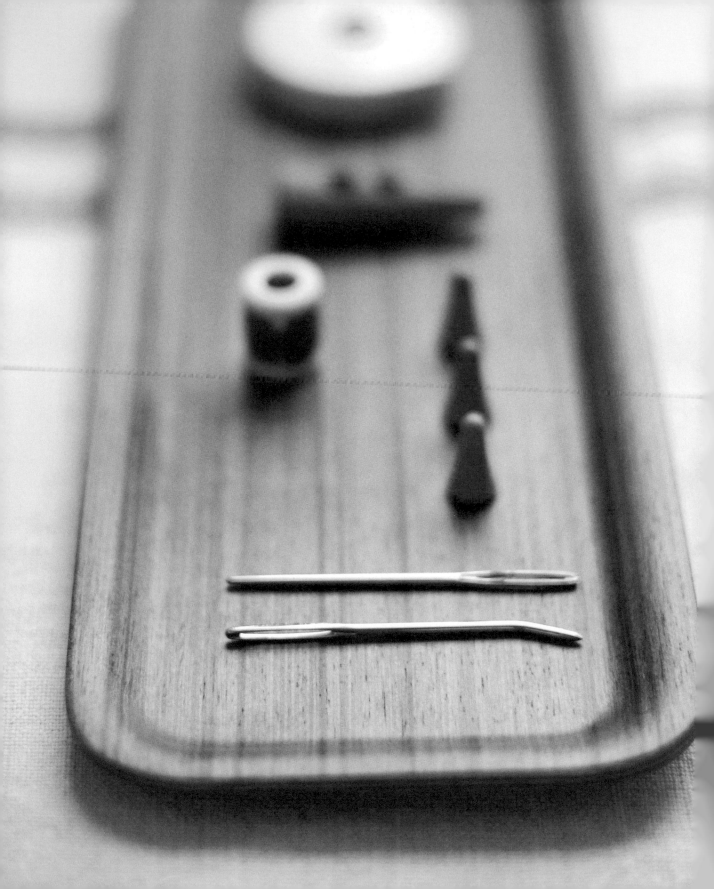

Acknowledgments

The best part of being a knitter is the community I've built around me and the friends with whom I share knitting and other joyous moments in life. So it's not surprising that the best part of writing this book was the community that grew around it. Not only did I share the experience with so many talented and wonderful people, but I could never have done it without the expertise and patience of each and every one of them.

Melanie Falick had the vision to help me develop this concept and bring it to life. Liana Allday, editor extraordinaire, was more supportive than I can say, and always had a smile for me, even on the phone.

Jared Flood (aka Brooklyn Tweed) turned my designs into photographic works of art along with the help of Karen Schaupeter's keen eye for styling.

Susi Oberhelman, the book designer, melded photography, patterns, and essays into a truly beautiful guide to knitting for men.

Sue McCain, the primary tech editor, made sure my designs and patterns made sense and helped me turn each one into a sweater for any man in any gauge yarn. Véronik Avery's wonderful design sense finessed the Baseball Jersey into a thing of wonder. Robin Melanson, tech editor, lent a second pair of eyes to each pattern, crossing my t's and dotting my i's.

Barbara and Richard Fabian generously opened their sun filled, mid-century modern home for a fabulous photo shoot. Carter Donnell, Roy Beaton, Ryan Flood, Andrea Danese, Jess Piranian, Richard Fabian, and Kevin Honeycutt all graciously and beautifully modeled my designs for the photographs. Urban Outfitters generously contributed much of the non-knitted wardrobe

Dottie Graves, Barbara Fabian, Jody Lewanda, Mary Pocknett, Wannietta Prescod, and Mireille Holland all clicked their needles for weeks, producing some of the beautiful samples the models are wearing.

Susan Ginsburg at Writers House, my agent of 15 years, and her ubercompetent assistant Bethany Strout, have always had my back.

To all of you, a huge hug of thanks and adoration.